The Overlooked Expert

Turning Your Skills Into a Profitable Business

SARAH GERDES

RPM Publishing

Coeur d'Alene, Idaho

Library of Congress cataloging-in-publication data on file

978-1979881241

Printed in the United States of America

First American Edition, 2008

Second American Edition, 2017

11182017

Melissa White www.evolvingdesignstudios.com

P.O. Box 841 Coeur d'Alene, ID 83816

A PERSONAL MESSAGE TO YOU

10th Anniversary Edition

November 2017

Since the original Overlooked Expert was written in 2008, the predicted recession occurred and many individuals who were laid off fell into the unemployment or underemployment lines. Yet others, resourceful and enterprising, struck out on their own, taking their skills, knowledge and know-how to the world by starting a small business.

I didn't realize I was considered an expert until I was approached to manage a live event for a local college. One month later, I had started my own business, earning five times what I was making at my day job (a radio station), which I kept because I loved it. I was in my twenties, but because I started in radio at fifteen, I already had ten years' experience, more than a lot of owners. **Chuck Pryor, Executive director & producer, Joel Osteen Radio**

Today, we are on the verge of another downturn. Many are looking for an additional source of income, to supplement what they already earn or to protect against job loss. The time was right to revise and update a resource that has helped so many realize the dream of additional income at low or no startup costs.

This 10th anniversary edition of The Overlooked Expert takes you further and deeper into the details of twenty-four overlooked experts who realized their strengths and formed profitable businesses. In this revised edition, strategic insights, business rules, hard-earned wisdom, tips, and bullet-point lists to be followed and checked off have been added. All increase your chances of creating and operating a profitable business.

Some of the Overlooked Experts featured in this book such as Chuck Pryor, never attended college, while others have graduate degrees. Many continue to work full-time jobs while moonlighting in the off-hours to satisfy financial goals.

The ages, industries and careers vary, but they all have a few things in common. We (and I include myself in this category), all came to a point in our lives where we had an ***A-Ha* moment** and realized we could be doing more. Beyond the initial discovery of an overlooked skillset, we found a commonsense approach to determine if the skills had a value on the open market. The natural result was starting a business for little or no cost and realizing immediate income.

A little fearful or hesitant? You aren't alone. All of us were in the beginning. The stories shared have been done to help you gain the confidence you require and skip over the mistakes. As you gain knowledge and identify with the examples of others, it's my hope you will take that first step to a major life improvement now, and in the process, you will be better able to weather the economic ups and downs that will surely come again.

Let's get started.

--Sarah Gerdes

The Overlooked Expert

Turning Your Skills

Into a Profitable Business

Table of Contents

"With confidence, you have won before you have even started."

Marcus Garvey

Introduction

The day I was told it would take years to earn a promotion to senior management, I knew it was time to consider a different job or start my own business. I was twenty-six, had been a manager for three years, and was disillusioned and angry. Yet it gave me the life-jolt I needed to wake me up to my potential. My boss's revelatory double whammy of stating he wasn't going anywhere and the company needing to triple in revenue before we required another layer of management was what I required to get going, or face the likelihood I'd be in my position for years to come.

But I didn't have years. I had my upcoming wedding to help pay for and no time to lose.

I assessed my intellectual assets, and scoured the Internet for job openings. Sure enough, full-time roles were listed covering the areas of marketing, sales and business development within my skill set. I pitched one hiring manager on the benefits of employing me as a contractor instead of a full-time resource. Within a week, I was working after hours, at home to earn extra income. Thirty days and three projects later, I'd added an additional $7,500 to my checking account.

At the time, I felt relief I'd covered my portion of the wedding, and didn't have the capacity or desire to consider a job move. It wasn't until the honeymoon was over that I faced the reality that my career potential hadn't changed one bit. If I wanted a better income and control over my future, I needed to make a dramatic change, and failure wasn't an option.

My determination was matched with confidence in my abilities. Aside from my now regular side projects, I continued to use my skills for corporate employers launching products and creating revenue. Yet it wasn't until I went out on the open market, as it were, that I learned the true value of what was in my head.

Hidden skills and knowledge are the essence of a successful small business or consulting firm. Unleash and leverage what is locked inside your head to help others while helping yourself.

Fast Forward

Any resentment about my lack of upward mobility faded as I continued moonlighting during the evenings, deposited checks and made plans to eventually leave. It took me another four months to give my notice, because I needed to conduct market research, check out the competition, etc., but the result of my efforts paid off, and handsomely.

Three years after starting my own firm, Business Marketing Group (BMG), in San Francisco, revenue tripled every year to reach a million dollars. My firm was profiled in *Fortune Magazine*, *Inc. Magazine* and *Entrepreneur*, and I was invited to speak at Harvard, Stanford and other Ivy League Schools. My clients included start-ups and Fortune 500 clients alike, as well as the governments of Britain and Ireland. I even penned a book on growing businesses through partnerships for McGraw-Hill.

The Overlooked Expert is the person who's fully capable of starting and running a profitable business

---

My experience is not unique. Consider a few of The Overlooked Experts profiled within this book:

- A stay at home mom turned organizing consultant, earning $1,200 per month working within a twenty-mile radius of her home.
- A doctor who consults to the military and the technology industry earning over $75,000 in annual supplemental income.
- An attorney who works as an editorial consultant for fiction books who earns enough each year to pay for his 401K.
- A network IT specialist turned business IT strategy consultant, who equaled his former corporate salary by the end of year two.
- An automotive technician running a 10-person shop, but who wants to sock extra money away and hosts 2, 5-day workshops a month, earning an average of $14,000 per month in extra income.
- A family counselor turned dog consultant to veterinarians and universities who within three years became a leading expert in the US.
- A woman who turned her ability to train her puppy into a puppy training business. She now grosses $350,000 per year between puppy training, boarding and product sales.
- A human resources staff member who became a resume consultant, maintaining his income, but enjoying the flexibility of working from home.
- A former restaurant general manager who now creates marketing programs for small businesses in multiple industries while working a

day job as a GM for a medical services company, earning nearly $50,000 in three years in her "off-time."

Without exception, each had a moment of truth, or a tipping point, that made them say: "I have to do this!" The following experience was the *A-Ha* idea that evolved into the actual service offered.

Is this book for you?

This book is for the individual who wants to earn more income, but hasn't yet taken the first step. It's also for the person who has already made the decision and perhaps completed a project or two and needs help building referrals, hiring staff or increasing profits on earnings.

I'm writing for those who are still being overlooked by business schools, experts, and authors because we are the silent majority of people who can moonlight our way to success, on our terms, from home (and later, an office if desired) and fulfill our financial and personal goals.

Within these pages are success stories for every aspect of a sole proprietor to establish and grow his or her business. Alongside these are examples of mistakes and missteps: highlighting failures can be helpful in pointing out scenarios and decisions to be avoided. *The Overlooked Expert* contains plenty of instances of both.

Book Organization

Chapter One: The Overlooked Expert

Chapter One begins with the commonsense approach others used to identify, list and categorize learned intellectual capital. Sources, typical earning power and pitfalls of selected professions are shared along the way, painting a picture of a future life as a business owner.

Chapter Two: Choosing a Niche

Not all businesses based around a person's knowledge are created equal. Some are more profitable, easier to grow and manage than others. This chapter focuses on evaluating the market needs, and how to map this with knowledge and skills to determine a niche.

Chapter Three: Defining your Services

People understand the dinner options on a Chinese menu, but that's not always the best way to offer consulting services. Chapter Three focuses on defining your business in terms that can be easily understood and sold. It also covers the tools that you can use during the sale and most importantly, how to guarantee client satisfaction.

Chapter Four: Making Money aka Getting Paid

Getting the highest return for your knowledge is vital. Chapter Four includes advice on structuring fees, retainers, commissions and when to use hourly and project rates. It also covers trades for services, choosing a location for a business, and what type of name will best serve your market and best communicate your services.

Chapter Five: Telling Your Story

You may have the greatest service in the world, but firms can't hire you if they don't know about you. Chapter Five includes strategies for creating awareness and demand for your new business, while prevent "over-demand," an especially risky situation that is behind small business failures.

Chapter Six: Methodologies and Best Practices

You don't have to be a global business to benefit from tracking, recording, and honing the process of the "how's" of your business. Chapter Six describes why service-based businesses use methodologies to increase revenue and margins and ensure that each client project delivers high-quality results.

Chapter Seven: Getting the Most from Your Team

Growing your business will push your resources and staffing requirements. You can backlog clients, limit engagements, hire full-time employees or contractors. Chapter Seven covers all your options along with incentives to retain quality personnel.

Chapter Eight: Growing Your Business

Becoming a consultant is half the battle. The other half is positioning yourself as an expert to grow your business. Chapter Eight includes strategies to improve your revenue by building your expert status credentials and convert your knowledge into a physical or electronic product.

Chapter Nine: Partnering for Success

Smart partnerships are one way to maintain the growth of a company, bring new products to market, open new distribution channels, or even lower the cost of goods sold. Chapter Nine explains the benefits and pitfalls of partnerships, and how to prepare yourself in case of a sale, merger, or failure of a business or the partnership itself.

Chapter Ten: Moonlighting Your Way to Success

You may not want to leave a well-paying job during good or bad times in order to start a consulting firm. Guess what? You may not have to. Chapter Ten provides proven strategies for approaching your boss about consulting on the side, and when you can potentially consult full-time, offering your services back to your employer.

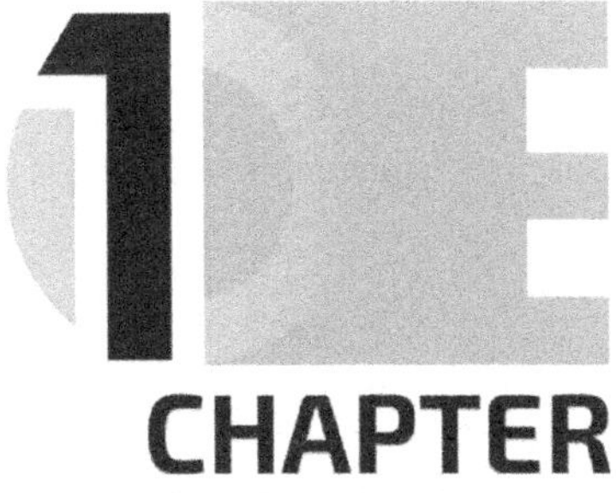

CHAPTER

The tipping point is that magic moment when an idea, trend, or social behavior crosses a threshold, tips, and spreads like wildfire.

— **Malcolm Gladwell,**

The Tipping Point: How Little Things Can Make a Big Difference

Chapter One: Leaving Is Freeing

Just after the conversation with my boss, I remember looking around at others in my position, holding my same title and realized a certain truth: **Middle managers are essential but many times get stuck in a role for years.** They—we—you, are the Overlooked Experts who create strategy and tactically implement programs. Sometimes, middle managers are confined because the person above isn't about to retire any time soon (as with my case). Other times, the person is deemed *too valuable* to be promoted into senior management.

- She's a marketing staff member who develops perfect web sites but is stuck because a role with broader responsibility isn't available.

- He's a project manager passed over time and time again for a job promotion due to management's laziness in training or hiring another (costlier) person.
- She's an employee who works her way up from manager to director yet her salary is never in sync with her position.

I'd wager these individuals are the people who know the business better than anyone, understand the language and mindset of the customers and can start a consulting firm and be profitable within sixty days.

Are you an Overlooked Expert? Consider if any of these descriptions apply to you:

- ✓ You have a specific skill set that enables you to create a strategy or plan and implement it from beginning to end.
- ✓ You are self-directed and require little or no oversight to accomplish your job.
- ✓ You can think up solutions to problems within a given field, provide a plan, and then do the work.
- ✓ You know how to uncover problems, provide guidance, and manage conflict.
- ✓ You are good at conflict resolution when it arises among people in different groups; you can keep the contributors focused on the solution to the point of positive resolution.
- ✓ You are detailed on follow-through after a task or project is completed, gaining validation that all parties are pleased.

- ✓ You have a knack for details; you can send out project completion notices, sign-up materials, and invoices.
- ✓ You can spot opportunities for improvement in any setting and are energized by providing solutions.
- ✓ You are trustworthy, you do your work and others who work with you rely upon you when the going gets tough.

It's not necessary you have every trait listed before you launch out on your own. It's more important to understand the value of each attribute, and not shy away from developing your capabilities.

Determination and discipline are the most important characteristics of a successful entrepreneur

---

Self-Realization

A good friend works in sales for a company providing project management services for overseas manufacturing. When she decided it was time to look for a new job, she called for my advice. She was concerned her résumé wasn't on par with her contemporaries because she'd taken five years off to have children. I explained that five years off didn't negate her three years of experience, nor did it diminish her existing role.

Still, she was dubious.

"But everyone has three to five years' sales experience," she feared, implying that she was on the low side of the time requirement scale.

She was also concerned that the skills she had didn't set her apart from others in her field.

I decided to take her through a ***skills assessment exercise***. I asked about her day-to-day activities. The dialogue went something like this:

"Haven't you been managing a team of twelve overseas?" I asked. She responded in the affirmative. "Once the client was signed, didn't you handle the project management?" Also, an affirmative. "Doesn't that entail taking the product from concept, through testing and quality assurance and delivery?"

"Of course," she replied. "We provide a single point of management for the client."

"And haven't you been responsible for blogging, managing the website content, identifying and selecting the e-mail marketing databases, writing newsletters, and placing ads?"

After fifteen minutes of this kind of back and forth, she had a moment of self-realization. She ceased to view herself as "only" a sales person. Her expanded awareness included many facets of marketing, including events, public relations, advertising, and then into the areas of hiring, training, project and program management. She also knew about creating partnerships and developing sales programs.

After she had her personal *A-Ha* Moment, I proceeded to point out that she could take on two or three clients, work from home and earn double what she made working for an employer.

This is exactly the kind of conversation an overlooked expert might have that leads to seriously considering starting a small business.

All it takes is the tipping point of frustration to open the door of opportunity.

Take Jared Redick, founder of The Résumé Studio, (www.theresumestudio.com). As a résumé consultant, Redick works one-on-one with clients to write highly targeted job-search documents. (Working directly with the end-customer is called Business to Consumer, or B2C). This might seem like a service that falls in to the category of: He makes money doing *that*?

Now consider this vocation from another angle, that of the consumer. If you are seeking a job, wouldn't you want the expertise and insight from an insider assisting with your résumé creation, from what to place on the résumé, in what order, and even the style for a certain industry and job specialty to better your chances of getting a job?

The answer to all those questions is: "Of course!" and that's what Jared banked on when he started his business. Industries have styles, just as HR managers prefer certain formats for different job titles (I wasn't previously aware of that little nuance). Jared knows details like this that the rest of us overlook or don't know exist. He makes his insight available by the hour or by the project to fit a budget. To top it off, Jared provides free templates for those with micro (or non-existent) budgets.

What seems like a silly idea for a services niche is, in reality, an extremely profitable vocation. Three hundred million people work in the United States, with an average unemployment rate of 4.9% or eight million people. If even a fraction of these individuals use a résumé consultant, the revenue numbers can be quite healthy.

Have you been a human resource manager and know what constitutes a put together resume? Are you even better at creating on-line resumes, posting or spotting good job candidates? Were you aware that many companies employ consultants to review and filter resumes? Perhaps you could be a consultant in the human resources industry.

Going to the Dogs

Nothing could be further from résumé consulting than perhaps puppy training. Not dog training, mind you, puppy training.

Becky Bishop, CEO of Puppy Manners (www.puppymanners.com) had her *A-Ha* moment for a puppy-training business when existing dog-training firms refused to accept her three-month-old puppy, a black Labrador named Magic.

Although Becky had no formal training in the field, she'd attended hundreds of hours of training for older dogs. She felt that she had enough expertise in the area to train her own animal, and through discipline and determination, she did. After a few months, she was receiving compliments from veterinarians, fellow dog owners and even the local dog trainers who had turned her down. One day, Becky realized she had a talent, and that she was herself, an overlooked expert in puppy training.

Becky distinctly remembers it as her *A-ha* moment. It occurred when she was looking down at Magic and she wondered why so many dog-training facilities focused on animals five months old and not younger? Now that she'd done it herself, she knew it was possible.

She looked at Magic's little black face, pulled the Kleenex out of her mouth, and told her: "Magic, you and I will build a business helping people with puppies."

That was it. Becky started her business because she wanted to help families with children raise a well-mannered dog.

One wouldn't think training and consulting go hand in hand, but they do. She trains the puppies (and the dog owners are her clients) while she consults—through education—the individuals and organizations who refer her business. Unlike Jared Redick, who consults and provides services exclusively to consumers, Becky does both Business to Consumer (B2C) and Business to Business (B2B). Wearing her "consultant hat," she educates other businesses, the veterinarians, dog breeders and animal retailers who give advice to dog owners. In this capacity, she performs all the duties of a consultant in a professional services role: educating, coaching, training, assessing and more. She is one of those service providers who relies upon and works with both businesses and customers.

Becky's efforts paid off. Within three years, gross earnings were $60,000, and by year five, had reached approximately $350,000. By that time, she had added boarding and product sales to her business, both natural outcroppings (and requests) from her clients. She extended her "products" as she calls them, organically, but it is her training of the puppies that's her core business and differentiator and the referrals through her consulting efforts that remain constant through the economic ups and downs.

Assessing Your Intellectual Capital

You are reading this book because you are venturing out on your own or know someone who is. Future business owners, particularly those using their knowledge, are called consultants, because they aren't selling a physical product. In this arena, it is the service you are selling, and so the phrase 'consultant' is often used. That said, you will read that not all individuals refer to themselves as a consultant. Sometimes it's a trainer, advisor or subject matter expert. For the purposes of simplicity, I'm going to use the general term of consultant.

The first thing a consultant needs to do is assess the knowledge and skills they have in a particular area. This knowledge is commonly referred to as intellectual capital and encompasses the information that one has about any subject, such as the context, issues, challenges, or solutions. Open *Fortune Magazine*, and you'll read how F500 CEO's consider intellectual capital to be one of the most important assets of the business. That's why they are reluctant to let top-flight talent go.

Yet, we are witnessing mass layoffs, be it JC Penny or Macy's, who closed a total of nearly a thousand stores in 2017, or Lowes, which let go nearly 1,400 people, 500 in management alone.

How many of those individuals were prepared for the pink slip? And of those, how many do you believe could start up their own business, relying upon the know-how and knowledge they have gained? You will read about several in the retail space who did just that!

Reader time out: Three words are critical. One word is going to be your mantra, your light on the dark road, and that's **Confidence**. You may be let go because of financial reasons, but that doesn't alter your abilities. Your **Competence** doesn't fade, even though your job has. This is where **Belief** comes into play. Your confidence, competence, and belief will sustain you through the fear, uncertainty and doubt. Knowing with everything you are, that you can do it. Others have done it and so can you.

As the example of my friend in sales illustrates, going through the skills assessment exercise alone dramatically improved her confidence. Once she was done, and she fully absorbed the depth and breadth of her intellectual capital, her outlook for a new career dramatically improved.

Like Becky, it was easy for my friend to overlook her skill set in sales and project management---but why? Because in both areas, the basic skills and acumen came naturally. So much so, that it was nearly dismissed as ordinary. We'll delve into that aspect later, but for now, focus on the opportunity and reason for change.

Where are you at with your present situation? Do you have an imminent event, like a wedding, or is it opportunistic, because you are receiving so many comments on your training abilities, like Becky?

While Becky was speaking with veterinarians, I was pulling up Craigslist (www.craigslist.com) to help categorize my list of skills. Because I didn't have the correct names for a few of my capabilities, (and wasn't sure whether they were all that valuable anyway), I looked up positions, the associated compensation and replicated the terms the hiring manager used on the ad.

As I was going through Craigslist, related tasks appeared that I'd done but had totally forgotten about. One area was product packaging. Over the years, I'd worked with designers and vendors to create may types of packaging, from software to consumer products such as music. It had been a few years, but my knowledge was still fresh and relevant.

Another area was collateral development. Today, most companies offer a digital form of a product sheet or brochure, but thousands of industries still print collateral for distributors or large customers who want to take notes or put a physical copy in their file. I began jotting down all the product lines I'd been responsible for managing, and the associated written, electronic and video collateral, managing a half-dozen agencies and multi-million-dollar budgets.

Reader time out: Were you a secretary or assistant at a job, wherein you wrote text for advertisements or copy for a brochure or three? What about materials for the sales reps? Have you created a presentation for the executive team? These are all forms of collateral development, which fall under the Marketing Communications category. To the degree you created, contributed, edited and produced these items, you can count those as skills you created 'on the job,' all of which have a very real monetary value.

Insider tip: If you are thinking about switching vocations or branching out on your own, use Glassdoor.com to find average salaries. It lists national averages as well as city-by-city. It also has a search feature that offers up categories and options in case you aren't sure.

A Business Based on Flexibility & Food

Erika Spry thought she'd work in the food industry through high school and college, but get "a real job," the minute she received her degree.

"Funny how different our vision and our life ends up," she said with a smile.

Erika recounted her journey, which started in the food and beverage industry, first, as a fifteen-year-old hostess. As she aged and grew in experience, her roles evolved to waitress, then as a bartender as a college student.

"It was good money and I had no incentive to stop." By the time she was in her early twenties, she had learned every aspect of the operations, including menu development, marketing, hiring and training. At twenty-five, her short-term, "filler-job turned in to a career" when she was promoted to the position of general manager. The store was grossing a half-million in revenues, and she was the youngest director of marketing in its history.

Before she jumped another rung on the restaurant ladder, she got drafted into the catering side of the business, and before she knew it she was working in entertainment.

"It started out because we were catering these huge stadium events, which meant musicians and groups." A few years into the job, she was recruited into another related industry; the analysis and editorial niche, covering the trends, revenues, demographics and ticket purchasing information. She learned how to gather data, set ticket prices, understand the volumes and discounts of every type of entertainer and venue. A part of this was connecting the entertainer with the ticket price, the experience and yes, even the food.

One year, Erika found herself at the annual awards ceremony for the producers of the biggest stars.

"They weren't the famous people," she confided. "But they are the people who control every aspect of the industry—the silent power players." She'd earned her way to being with this elite group, and looked back on her nearly twenty-year history in awe.

"I really couldn't believe it had all happened organically."

Seasoned and well-paid, she was by this time, also married. When she became pregnant, her life took another turn.

"I looked at everything I knew *how* to do and then thought about what I *wanted* to do. I wanted the flexibility to take on the clients that fit with my schedule."

Erika knew life on the road as a traveling executive, staying out late entertaining her clients was incompatible with her vision of motherhood. With over three thousand cookbooks in her home, she went back to her first love: food.

She decided to start a B2B restaurant consultancy, with herself as the one and only employee. She'd also moved from California to Coeur d'Alene, Idaho, a small city about thirty minutes from Spokane, Washington.

"I wasn't sure what kind of response I'd get, so I started putting the word out with my hairdresser, next door neighbor, my nail person—anyone I came in contact with."

"It turned out that those individuals weren't necessarily the person who owned the business or ran the restaurant, but all of them had friends who did."

Within the first three years, she earned roughly fifty-thousand dollars part time, working the hours she wanted, and around her young daughter, and from home.

"It was the perfect situation for someone in my position, because I chose the projects that fit my schedule, and it didn't cost me anything to start. No overhead or office space."

And it all came from word of mouth. "People were always asking for advice anyway, so this was a natural transition to paying clients."

Intellectual Capital Cheat Sheet

- ✓ Create a list of your skills and job know-how
- ✓ Organize the list into categories by job division or functional area (e.g., marketing, sales, or operations)
- ✓ Sort it again by selecting those jobs you can start and finish
- ✓ Circle items where you have managed internal or external resources
- ✓ Mark or highlight the projects that can be publicly referenced
- ✓ Create a timeline for approaching the list

Your Service and the Company Name

Attorneys and doctors benefit from using their own name as the business name. Yet, this can work against a consultant whose own clients are other businesses, as opposed to consumers.

When it comes right down to it, the little impressions a consultant makes, from the name of the company to the corporate pitch, are important to each prospect. Consider six things you can build a name around and see which one fits your industry and your business, but also may differentiate you from the competition.

Six options for creating a name for your business

- What you do (Greenspace House Restoration Consulting)
- Who you are (John Stanford Tax Business Consulting)
- What industry you serve (Fast Resume Consulting Design)
- The area in which you live (Chicago Beauty Consultants)
- How you differentiate yourself (Best Editorial Services)
- Your competitive positioning (Top Shelf IT Consulting)

Based on the advice of a friend, I chose a name that could be shortened. Business Marketing Group (BMG) sounded like a large company. So much so, that many people would remark, "Haven't I heard of that before?" In fact, many of them had—it was called Bertelsmann Music Group, and I'd joke that if I was the CEO of that company, I probably wouldn't be there, talking with them in person.

It invariably broke the ice, but it wasn't until a few years of consistent press coverage that the firm got recognized on its own.

Ten consulting vocations

Have you worked in marketing or for a marketing firm? You might consider becoming an:

1. **Event Management Consultant**: consults clients on identifying, selecting, creating and staging events, from industry trade shows to birthday parties, weddings, or sales meetings.
2. **Product Packaging Consultant**: consults on creating the best packaging for a product, be it food packaging, bike parts, clothing, earrings, or beauty accessories.
3. **Public Relations Consultant**: consults other businesses (such as new PR agencies) on setting up best practice operations, billings etc., but could also consult to clients that are internal corporate communications departments.
4. **Advertising Consultant**: consults other agencies on the latest methods, trends and programs to create awareness. Could also consult to individuals or small businesses who are unable to afford a boutique or large advertising agency.
5. **Product Marketing Consultant**: consults entrepreneurs and small businesses on establishing a product marketing team, the product development life cycle, methods for product, focus groups and consumer testing.

6. **Outsource Manufacturing Consultant**: consults small businesses desiring to outsource product manufacturing.
7. **Speaker Bureau Consultant**: consults prospective speakers on the right forums and speaking venues for a subject, industry or vocation.
8. **Organizational Consultant**: consults families or businesses on the best use of space.
9. **Boutique Retail Consultant**: consults on a specialty area of retail, such as unique children's apparel and accessories, for a demographic or regional market.
10. **Business and IT Consulting Services:** consults clients on the best way to align business goals with the technical software and services required to achieve those goals.

Action Items: Stage 1

- Evaluate your situation: Are you an overlooked expert?
- What is your area(s) of expertise?
  - List them, by category
  - Get as detailed as you can
- Are you interested in adding to your income on a part-time basis?
- Does your area of interest allow you to work at odd times of the day (or night) when the house is quiet and you can still be getting work done?

- Are you ready to extend yourself to use all that you have learned up to this point?
- Do firms advertise for the skill set you have?
- Have you looked at job postings to get an idea of how to present your skills?
- How broad is your network of friends, work colleagues, or church or affiliation associations who could assist your efforts?
    - How many referrals do you think each one can bring?
- Do you have a friend that compliments your skill set, and may be a potential partner?
- Are you ready to commit to yourself that today is that day to assess your future?

Congratulations. You've made it past the first stage, which is filled with a lot of questions. Some of those should be answered by now, and with confidence. It's time to move to Stage 2.

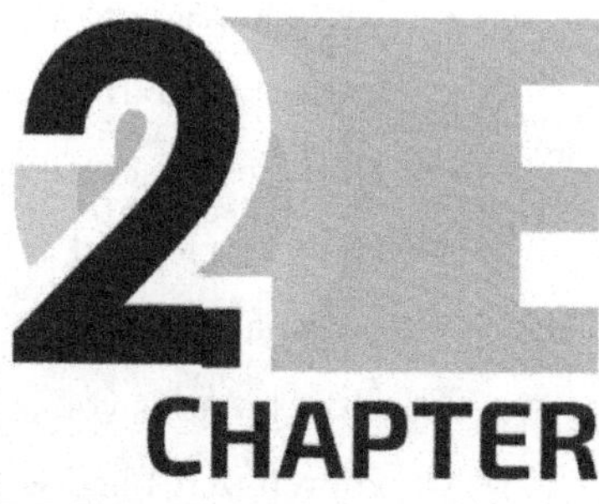

CHAPTER

Consultants must find a niche and stick to it. If you can't find one, create one.

Tim Bajarin, Analyst, Futurist, Creative Strategies, Contributor, Time Magazine

Chapter Two: Choosing a Niche

Bryan Kelley is a forty-year old owner of Valley Automotive based in Covington, Washington. From an early age, he was under the body of a car, working alongside his father. By the time he was a teenager, he was employed at the local Ford dealership, and by twenty-two, was earning as much as men thirty years his senior. Bryan can't remember a time when he wasn't working on a car.

"It was just what I did," he said modestly. As an automotive technician, he could fix nearly any car brought to him "except exotics," and most of the autos at his father's shop and at the dealership were American made. He loved to educate others, so he took a two-year break to teach high school students, hoping to endow teens with a passion for fixing cars.

That was when he had his first *A-Ha* moment.

"When I went to teach high school automotive classes, I thought I'd blend the love of what I did for a living with teaching, and it would be perfect."

Reality was different than his vision, and after twenty-four months, he left to go back to the dealership. "I loved the teaching part but hated the politics. I knew that public service wasn't for me, and I needed to stay in the private sector."

While he was "welcomed back with open arms," at the dealership, he grew increasingly frustrated. "I kept wondering why I was getting paid so little when the customer was being charged a hundred dollars and hour." When he turned twenty-four, Bryan began moonlighting at two local automotive shops. During this time, he had his second *A-Ha.*

"I knew I had the skills to do the work, and thought I could eventually run a business." With that objective, Bryan saved for three years to purchase one of those shops, spending half a million dollars for the building and land, using a combination of cash and financing. "My own ignorance led me to do that." The consequence? "I didn't sleep for three years."

Like many first-time business owners, he had ups and downs. The ups included a lot of revenue. But by the end of year four, he was $120,00 in debt with outstanding bills to vendors, suppliers and the bank. He only had $1,200 in his accounts but cash was still coming in. "I knew how to take care of cars, hire people and manage customers," he said. "What I didn't know how to do was run the business."

Bryan's fortunes turned around when two things happened. The first is he employed a consultant to help him learn the business and operations side (that alone is an interesting niche- helping other small businesses). In sixteen months, Bryan altered his operations so dramatically that he paid off his entire debt, and made a small profit. (Later in the book, Bryan's pricing strategy, marketing and community efforts are detailed, because it's a case study in what to do, how long it takes and the payoff). "I didn't realize I made more profit in year one than years two-through-four combined."

Then Bryan had his third *A-Ha* moment: he could teach others what he knew, get paid for the knowledge he had, thereby becoming an automotive repair consultant to the private market.

"My love of educating never went away, but it had to take a backseat, literally and figuratively, to running my company. But eventually I added consulting to my business, and that's when things really took off."

Business owner to consultant

Bryan had a contact in the automotive trainer certification business who had approached him about the quality of Bryan's work and his reputation in the community. Bryan encouraged this conversation and ended up being selected as one of a handful of trainers in Washington State for automotive technicians who require certifications. When I brought up the notion of the overlooked expert to Bryan, he laughed.

"Yes and no," he said. "On one hand, I knew I was good at cars, but it came so naturally, I never thought of it as a skill set, so yes, I had overlooked myself. On the other hand, the value of owning and running a business for a few years is that I started to get a picture of the value of what was in my head, but it wasn't until that information was narrowed and focused in a specific way that it became tangible—as in, I could do it and make money at it."

He was talking about the consulting niche of automotive training certification. Automotive was the industry, training was the consulting specialty, and certification within that was the niche. Within that was a subspecialty. "Used cars, not exotics or high-end autos where the owners will typically go to the dealer."

Initially, he thought the market for consulting would be rather small. On this, he was pleasantly surprised.

"I had no idea how large the market was until I held my first seminar." The attendance rose from single to double digits within the first few months. Here are the details.

- **Unique and custom content**

Bryan's "seminars," are of his own making; the content, format, structure and everything in between, were all designed by him. He typically updates the information once a month, always looking for the newest techniques, state and local requirements or annotations to the industry and even new parts to bring in.

- **Condensed and convenient**

After playing around with formats and structure, he settled on five days a week, five hours a day, thereby giving the most information in the shortest period of time, without tapping into the weekend schedule of most technicians.

- **Self-hosting or renting**

A small class is 8, and a large one is 40. Anything thing under 20, Bryan can host at his building which he owns. When the group is larger, he will rent a local facility.

- **Smart pricing and high value**

Charging $325 per person for the five-day course, Bryan grosses between $2,600-$13,650. The amount charged is a lot less than some groups but more than others. Bryan has a philosophy that sits well with his mostly packed classes.

"We give them twenty hours of training and it's not watered down. It's data and technique, as well as how to apply it. Plus, we feed them every night," he says proudly. "**In an industry where every fifteen minutes counts for real dollars** saved on the part of both the technician and the customer, or a single bolt saves a couple bucks, **you are talking a huge savings for most car centers.** If you can give a person just one piece of information that saves fifteen minutes, times that by twelve a month and you have paid for the class." In fact, Bryan's data gathering has shown that the cost of the seminar returns itself in thirty days, and that many of the technicians are from competing shops.

- **Feed them**

Bryan's wife makes homemade food so the attendees don't have to go hungry and the group doesn't have to take a break to go off site. A buffet is set up, the attendees fill their plates and Bryan keeps talking. "It's fast, efficient and it's great food!"

As Bryan's primary business grew, so did his consulting. His annual automotive repair business now grosses between $1.3-1.6M in a new building with ten bays and four full-time employees. On the other hand, his consulting business employs one person, himself.

"My wife benefits in other ways," he says with a smile. It's that business, he emphasizes, that is providing for his savings, his vacations and other discretionary items.

Bryan's reputation for training and knowledge has grown over the years, and the number of seminars given per year has kept pace. "We held twelve seminars last year and this year, we will hold probably 20-22." That's a seminar nearly every other week of the year, all year around.

"Anyone can do this type of thing," Bryan contends. "All it takes is hard work, and getting in there and doing it. And it's not just the automotive industry. Nearly any industry, and the individuals within that industry, can be helped or bettered. **You must isolate a niche, and then get in there and do it**. Because If you want to win at the game, you have to get in and play it."

If you want to win at the game, you have to get in and play it.

Bryan Kelley, CEO, Valley Automotive

Finding Your Niche

Bryan's case illustrates one simple point: think about alternatives beyond your present state. Bryan had never considered teaching or training once he opened his business; it was an industry professional that noticed his work, knew of his reputation and approached him to ascertain his interest level. It was only in hindsight that he processed the market, and connected the dots from his knowledge and skills to a market niche that wasn't narrow at all; it was more than enough to bring him tens of thousands of dollars in extra income per year.

A simple exercise

- Start with the industry you know
- Create a column, or list, for each primary industry
- Segment this into sub-industries
    - medical industry
    - medical equipment
    - heart equipment etc.
- What is your area of specialty within this niche? Operating the equipment, as a product representative, marketing professional, customer support, technician/repairs
- Can you make a business providing services in the areas of your expertise, to either businesses or consumers?
- Does this niche have a name, are others providing services to this niche? (This identifies if it's an established area)
- Can you utilize your existing employer, partners, vendors or suppliers if you start up a business?

The demographics of the customer within the niche is key. After years in the automotive repair business, serving a clientele in a twenty-mile radius, Bryan had a good idea of his typical client demographic. E.g. age, income etc. Yet this had zero applicability when it came to his consulting business: instead of owners of cars, he was targeting the repair technicians. Bryan elected to spend his time ramping up his activities within the automotive repair industry itself (which he'd not done before) and this is detailed in later sections on marketing and awareness. Suffice it to say he attended a lot of industry events, got his name out to potential attendees and accelerated the growth of his secondary business.

> The U.S. Small Business Administration (SBA) provides a Small Business Readiness Assessment Tool that prompts you with questions to assist in evaluating skills, characteristics and experience as they relate to starting a business. The responses are scored and the profile is provided when you click submit. http://web.sba.gov/sbtn/sbat

Creating a Niche

Like Bryan and others who start a small business, I was doing two jobs at once. And while I was pleased with the ease and money of the first three contractor jobs, I wasn't convinced it was time to leave my job, and the source of my fear was my lack of differentiation. Did the world really need one more marketing specialist, I wondered?

Seeking reassurance, I called an analyst whom I'd met with many times over the years, Tim Bajarin.

Tim had started his own consulting firm five years before we met, when he was one of hundreds of analysts in the Bay Area reviewing and writing about technology. Today, he is a contributor to Time Magazine, and is considered one of the leading "futurists," in the US. When he started his firm, he differentiated himself by focusing on the then-new area of pen-based technologies, absorbing anything and everything about pen-based software, hardware, and mobile device trends. Soon, he was writing conclusions that proved to be spot-on. Bajarin's trend-watching made news, landing him as a reference in leading business publications like *Fortune* and *Inc. Magazine*, and he became an oft-quoted talking head on television and radio shows.

I'd watched Tim's rise from individual analyst to recognized authority, so I was interested in the pearls of wisdom he might give to another would-be consultant. "How had he differentiated himself from hundreds of consultants in the Bay area, and across the US?"

He took my phone call, and after hearing my pitch about my own marketing services, and asking a few questions about my background, he used the bluntness that made him an interviewer's favorite.

"Consultants must find a niche and stick to it. If you can't find a niche, then create one." That's what he had done, he said. Created a niche for himself in the pen-based area. That led to other—greater—things once his expertise was established.

After the call, I ruminated on his words. Those two sentences were the most useful and perplexing bit of advice I ever received. It made sense, but I didn't know which niche to select; I had roughly the same level of skill in different areas. On top of that, in San Francisco, a sales and marketing consultant seemed to exist on nearly every street corner. No skill I possessed differentiated me from the other person (or so I thought) except that I had called at the right time and offered a good price point.

Tim reminded me that when he had started covering mobile computing, the market niche itself was very new, and few (if any) of the established consulting firms, such as Gartner, Forrester and IDC, had assigned an analyst. They'd thought the market was small and insignificant, and didn't predict (as he did) that pen-based technologies were going to be the gateway to what would eventually become mobile-handheld devices. In other words, it was the advent of the smart device, which led to smart phones.

Tim recalled how he was determined to be one of the first consultants out of the gate, and in his case, he had the opportunity to coin the term "pen-based computing," which caught on, and was discussed for a decade until the stylus became a common product feature. While the trend of "pen-based computing" eventually phased out, he was forever seen as the leader in field.

While I admired Tim's foresight, I needed a personal breakthrough, and had no choice but to hold on until I had a spark of lightening that would differentiate me. In the meantime, I kept my day job, and determined to moonlight on side projects until the something landed on my desk.

And one day, it did, literally. I still remember the scene. It was about two weeks following my conversation with Tim. I was sitting in my little hobbit-hole like office; imagine red brick on three sides, a sliding glass door and glass walls in front of me, all of us were independent consultants, renting a space and sharing the "conference room" in the common area. I was doing my duty, reading an industry paper.

The article focused on the challenges Microsoft was having recruiting new partners. Think back to the time when San Francisco was cool, Seattle not-so-much, and Microsoft wasn't getting the right type of companies to pay them a visit to Redmond, Washington. The mid-level manager from Microsoft was bemoaning the fact that he couldn't attract and qualify the right type of partners to work with his product group. Like a bolt of lightning, I finally had my *A-Ha* moment.

Don't wait for the inspiration to find you. Begin, and one day you will find the inspiration.

H. Jackson Brown Jr.

Spotting a Market

Why not help find companies that align with Microsoft's strategy? This manager, responsible for hundreds of partners and had a multi-million-dollar budget had just self-identified a problem he couldn't solve. My second thought was if Microsoft had issues finding the right partner, then certainly other large companies, in the technology industry and many others, suffered from the same issue.

Two days later, I called up Tim Krause, the industry manager at Microsoft, who was quoted in the article. He picked up on the first ring (in those days, one could cold-call into Microsoft with just a name).

I introduced myself, mentioning that I'd read about his challenge in finding companies who could be potential partners. I proposed the idea of assisting him in the process of identifying, selecting, and bringing forth firms that could help meet his departmental goals.

"How much will this cost me?" he asked.

"Nothing," I replied. "I'll be paid by the clients who I'm representing, and therefore won't have a conflict of interest." I told him all he'd need to do is take the time to tell me a bit about what he was looking for and then help our efforts through the process. It wouldn't be confidential information, but I'd be exposed to the vision and direction of the product team at a partner-level, so it was more than the average potential partner could get, and with more clarity about timelines, process and the like. In short, I'd have an insider's look at the process for qualification of the partner opportunity, along with secondary facets such as technical and financial due diligence.

"What have I got to lose?" he asked rhetorically. Shortly thereafter, I became a free extension of his efforts, much as associates looking out for referral opportunities.

That month, I gave notice to my employer, confident I could pay the bills by accepting freelance marketing projects as I proved out my business model. If my hunch proved correct, a new consulting niche would be established, and I'd have a unique differentiation from other consultants. **Worst case was it failed, and I'd go back to the corporate world or continue freelancing.**

Reader time out: Do you have exposure to industry knowledge that is publicly available, but hard to come by unless you are "in thick of things" or "in the know?" Perhaps you have been coaching executives in an industry niche, and are looking for a new challenge. Can your industry knowledge and skills apply to more than your own corporation? It might be time to consider a consultant vocation based upon your expertise and knowledge.

But what about creating a new business in an existing market? Isn't that like 'building a better mousetrap,' or creating one more pair of shoes in a world already chock-full of sneakers?

A new way of Speaking: A highway without Speed limits

Where one sees a dead end, another sees a freeway without a speed limit. That's what separates the entrepreneur or small business owner from the rest of the world.

This is how Bryan Caplovitz felt when he spotted a hole within the speaker bureau market. "It was an established market constrained by expensive intermediaries which needed to be eliminated."

Caplovitz had been frustrated in his own efforts to locate speaking opportunities that mapped with his expertise. He found that going through an intermediary such as a speaker's bureau was helpful, but time-consuming and very expensive to the paying client (the organization who hired him to speak). Caplovitz was also tired of navigating multiple bureaus segmented by subject matter, be it celebrities, athletes, motivational speakers, spiritual speakers, and just about every other category, including Star Trek impersonators. His gut told him that a better way of connecting speakers with venues must exist. When he found that it didn't, he had his *A-Ha* moment. He decided it *should* exist!

After pondering the issue, Caplovitz found a way to figuratively remove the speed limits on the speaking industry freeway. He would create and provide a tool to match speakers with potential speaking opportunities, and make money.

Not long after, Caplovitz founded Speakermatch.com. This site allows meeting planners to list their events and the speaker description at no charge. The speakers, on the other hand, pay a small, monthly fee for the right to look through the online leads, day or night, eliminating the need for a live, human being to conduct a manual search.

Caplovitz's positioned Speakermatch as a 24X7 source connecting speakers with opportunities, thereby establishing a new niche in an existing industry. Speakermatch quickly proved that it could collapse the hours, days or even weeks it took to match up the right speaker with the ideal organization. Ten years after he started his firm, it is considered the leader in this area, which has experienced steady, profitable growth.

Existing market, New niche

You may be intimately familiar with holes in your industry. Can you be the one to satisfy an area of need that everyone readily acknowledges but still exists? Here are a few starters to finding out:

- Delve deeper with peers, colleagues, partners & vendors
- Ascertain the real issues to validate your understanding (e.g. is the problem more complex than you originally supposed or can it really be addressed?)
- Is this an issue that can be solved by a consultant with expertise, such as yourself?
- What would this area/consulting vocation be called?

The first and most important first step towards success is believing we can succeed.

Nelson Boswell

The first one isn't always the hardest

Bryan told others in his network about Speakermatch, and soon organizations were listing available speaker slots on this site (for a fee). Once he had a few listings, he put the word out to speakers and shortly thereafter, the first agreement was made between speaker and opportunity. He had his first reference and his business had been validated.

In my case, I called two vice presidents who bought into the idea of hiring me to create strategic partnerships. I'd pitched the notion of "outsourced partner development" because I needed a name for the category I was creating. The analogy I used was comparing the outsourcing of manufacturing and software development: if one could outsource those truly strategic areas to others, why not partnerships?

They concurred.

Of course, I did offer a nice incentive: zero dollars up front. As an unproven commodity, **I offered to provide my services without a retainer, billing for my work upon completion of the project**. This meant no money out on their part and no risk. All they had to invest was the time it took to educate me on their product and strategic direction. The rest was up to me, from identifying the best potential partners, making the pitch, setting the meetings, handling the technical and financial due diligence—all of it. If we got to the stage of having in-person meetings, the client would pay for it, which was acceptable. The value proposition would be agreed upon by both parties.

One engagement lasted approximately three months, the other about two. For one San Francisco-based client, I created a joint development agreement (JDA) with Microsoft. The other Oakland, California-based client also included a joint development agreement, as well as an investment and strategic partnership with SAP. I'd done all the work, from the first pitch call, through the discussions and due diligence, to the contract negotiation and completion.

These clients paid my fees retroactively, (which were still a fraction of a full-time employee, about $3,500 per month vs. $10,000 of a full-time headcount). But I was a sole proprietor, my only costs of rent, phone and partial utility thanks to sub-leasing a one-room office in downtown San Francisco.

Incentives for the unproven consultant

Once you leave the safe shell of a corporate employer, you no longer benefit from the reputation of that entity. Sure, you may know how to do the job, but first client or two who will be paying your fee doesn't know if you can set up, manage, bill, provide services and then follow up in a professional, consistent and productive way. Further, you don't have references who can vouch for your ability to handle tough situations, resolve conflicts, interact with all levels of executives and a host of other things that you are likely to blink your eyes and say: "Yes! Of course, I can do those things. I've been doing them for years." That's good, but you haven't done it on your own, and for a business or individual who will be paying hard-earned dollars, what they see, think and feel is: This is risky.

How to entice the first few clients

- **Offer the first service free.** Yoga studios do this all the time. 3 classes, two weeks, whatever the offer to entice the customer.
- **Be up front**, say you need client references in exchange for the first project/service (which will be free). This is exclusive of hard costs (if you have them) such as printing, fees for the program, such as a conference room and other necessary expenditures.
- **Offer a discount or delayed billing**. You can do this 100% on the back-end, or interval payments based on easily identifiable milestones.
- **Offer to trade services.** Perhaps your ideal first client is very risk adverse, and tells you that any time wasted has a high opportunity cost. Then you must entice this individual with something else. Perhaps you have a side-hobby that has value. Offer to trade the service (e.g. you give said individual a service for little/no cost) and in return, that individual invests the time necessary to prove out your idea.

Home-based businesses: a nice second income

Now, let's look at something a little closer to home, literally. **Many small businesses are staffed with a single employee (you) who can keep costs low and profits high using a home office.** We are still talking about a consultant using their smarts, not a person creating a product.

I have a friend, Shari Kenyon, who's middle daughter, Laura King, moved to Washington, D.C. after she graduated from college and her husband accepted a job with a law firm. Laura elected to be a stay-at home mom, but as her children aged, she found not-working full-time challenging. One day, Shari informed me Laura had started her own consulting firm called Miss Organized (www.missorganized-va.com).

I visualized a person who consulted with large companies about organizational behavior.

"Oh no!" Shari said, laughing. "I'm talking about organizing someone's office or home. Laura started doing closets before it evolved into organizing households. Then one day, a couple asked her to organize their life, including their business, and she did!"

Much to Shari's delight, this was the same child who left books in disarray on the countertop, and never picked up her own clothes. Apparently, when Laura got married, her organizational gene kicked in. When visitors to her home commented on the lack of clutter and proficient use of space, the idea of becoming an organizational consultant was Laura's *A-Ha* moment. Both she and her husband had overlooked her expertise in this area. Once it was pointed out to her, she thought about her own dissatisfaction at home and she created a business.

Within twelve weeks, Laura was earning several thousand dollars a month on her own terms, doing something that came easily.

The Home-based Technologist

One final example of a person who successfully chose a market niche and works out of a home office is Mike Konesky, the founder and CEO of Spokane, Washington–based Results Northwest (www.resultsnw.com).

After graduating from Santa Clara University with a B.S. in Computer Science/Mathematics in 1987, he joined IBM Global Services as one of only two college graduates to be hired by the professional services group. He put in a five-year stint at IBM in different roles, from delivery to sales, before he and his former boss started a consulting company in San Jose, California. It was founded to provide systems management services to semiconductor and government industries in Silicon Valley.

His market analysis was on-the-job conventional wisdom, something that many consultants have if they acquired experience with a large company. Once he and his wife determined that Washington State would be their final destination, Mike validated the same set of services would be required in another city and state. **He contacted prospective clients, gave a high-level pitch, assessed the interest, and in the end, felt confident he could run a consulting firm himself in the new environment.** It was only a matter of time then, before he made the decision to move, and start his own consulting firm.

Before Mike Konesky had the opportunity to start his firm, however, he was recruited to Seattle by the software firm Onyx in "a job position and money I couldn't refuse." He set aside having a small business for a time, figuring, "I'd learn all I could about the market up in the Northwest and determine if it still made sense." In the meantime, he'd gather real, empirical data and create a network of potential clients.

Mike rose through the ranks to become Managing Consultant for the West Coast Group Consulting Manager. He also spent time at another consulting firm, Ascentium, where he was the Principal Consultant charged with starting a branch office in Spokane. By the time he finally left to start his own consulting firm, he had created a list of all the contacts he had at all the companies where he could market his services located in the Greater Seattle region. He had also run several scenarios, about best, mid and worst-case scenarios. He determined if he could get even a ten percent hit rate (his worst-case scenario) he'd hit his revenue goals.

When he did open his business, Mike said his revenue goals were met by month three, and his "long-term revenue goals" of three years were hit at month twenty. His experience, patience and knowledge had paid off.

Reader time out: Are you naturally gifted turning sheets of paper, old jeans and buttons into little journals? I have friends, one female, the other male, both in their fifties, who recently starting consulting others on turning odds and ends into products for profit (holding small seminars and private lessons). Each earns roughly twelve-hundred dollars a month, all the while having a life and working a full -time job.

Market Size:

Determine if there is a market for your business before you launch. Is it required to understand how many people want your service before you create a web site and get your business license? No, not necessarily, but it might be a good idea, if for no other reason than you have the peace of mind that comes from *knowing* the number of people who might hire and pay for your service rather than *guessing*.

Bajarin told me the market size might be enough to pay my rent, but not enough to build a business. His comment struck me and I thought about how I'd start ascertaining a market that I was trying to create.

Like most single-person shops, I didn't have the budget to hire a firm to research a new market for me, so I took the common-sense approach. I started by calling Tim Krause back and asking a few more questions.

- How many partners was his group trying to sign?
- How many partners did he think *all of Microsoft* was trying to sign?
- How did this compare with Microsoft's competitors?
- How did they go presently recruit partners?
- What were the highest priority partners?

Krause answered it was in the low thousands for just one product group. If I signed even a fraction of that amount as clients (I couldn't handle more than a few myself per month), for a few thousand dollars a project (not counting stock, commissions or bonuses) my business would be robust for years. I'd have the option to maintain a one-person shop or grow as I desired.

Next, I conducted my own, on-line search confirmed that *thousands* of Microsoft's target partners were located in the Bay Area, and within a fifty-mile driving radius of my home/office. As I lived downtown San Francisco, I could drive an hour in any direction to have prospect meetings and on-site discussions. As funny as it sounds, I stopped my market research then, comfortable with the numbers I'd found.

Driving Radius: a simple formula

If you aren't in a position to travel or don't have the desire, using a driving radius as a baseline isn't a bad way to start.

In the densely populated area of Virginia, just outside D.C., Laura King estimated she knew a hundred people through her church, and each one of them probably knew an additional twenty or more people within a *twenty-mile radius.* **Laura created a simple spreadsheet, including the names, referral sources and general area of her prospective clients.** From this, she determined her target market (e.g. potential customer base) was large enough to support her desired monthly income of $500 at a minimum up to several thousand dollars with an expected number of four clients. Her hypothesis was born out within the first three months, and she capped her client load to meet her schedule.

Understanding the market based on a driving radius

- Create your first draft marketing/client referral list

- Identify all the organizations, then individuals you can tell about your business
- Sort by location (city) and drive time (miles/or time in car)
- Refine the list to the realistic individuals you can contact
- Add a caveat for those individuals who may work/live in one area, but may know others who live or work near you
- Estimate a price for your services and run one or two scenarios:
  - Conservative: 1 in 10 referrals convert to client
  - Medium: 2 in 10 referrals convert to client
  - Optimistic: 3 in 10 referrals convert to client
- Go the next step and run another scenario: client referrals
  - From the above, if you receive 50 referrals, 5 convert into clients
  - 3 are happy and give you references + 2 more referrals for a total of 5 new clients
- Extrapolate this information and you will see that in a matter of a few months, you may have more clients than you could adequately handle. More on this topic later.

Analysis to Validation

When it comes to market research, sometimes, a simple phone call will do.

Becky Bishop backed up her initial finding by picking up the phone book, looking on-line, and began calling. Outside understanding the competition (none), the vets in the region (those she knew and those she didn't=total number), and guessing at the number of dog owners, Becky's market sizing loosely translated into a revenue number she believed worthwhile for her animal consulting business which were proven out (more on this later).

She recounted how she made dozens of calls to vets, all who had more than one hundred customers. When she called, she didn't rudely ask for numbers, she put herself in the position of a potential customer/patient and "gently worked the phones."

"Do you have anyone you refer to who could help me with my two-month-old puppy?" Most vets replied that they not only lacked a referral for her, but they couldn't even suggest a book to read. She then went about asking as many questions as she could relating to her market sizing exercise. It wasn't until the very end, when it was more than evident that a) a market existed, b) the vet had no referrals to give and c) they were as interested in a source for puppy training as she was in providing it, did Becky give the pitch. It went like this:

"If I can show you results in training a puppy, would you recommend my services?"

Each one replied an enthusiastic yes. One vet confided that so many clients have puppy behavior issues, that when a vet did find a trusted source in the training area, the vets shared the news with one another.

Once Becky felt that Magic's training was complete, she showed him to her vet, who had once before commented on Magic's good behavior. He happened to be her first referral source when Becky told him she was formally opening her own training business.

Until then, Becky had only loosely checked on pricing her services. She immediately learned the hourly and group rates of other trainers in the area. Instead of undercutting the competition, she decided she would charge a little more than her established competitors.

"Why start at the bottom?" Becky asked herself. To her, lowball pricing made no sense. "I needed people to think I was better, and if it's better, it's going to cost more." Becky was gratified to learn that having a vet refer her services increased the credibility and justification for her fees.

Becky's vet referred the first client, a dark Labrador retriever named Barker. The puppy was successfully trained, the owners thrilled, the vet was pleased, and she had her first client referral. Her business was on its way.

Understanding the market of your professional referral sources (e.g. other businesses)

- ✓ Are they working with others offering your same services?
- ✓ Would they be interested in your brand of services?
- ✓ Understand the number of clients/customers for each referral source
- ✓ Identify who they presently use (if anyone)
- ✓ Search the Internet for those names provided
- ✓ How many exist?
- ✓ What do they offer and charge?
- ✓ What will you offer that's unique and most importantly….
- ✓ Is the market big enough to support another consultant in your area?

Maslow's Hierarchy of Needs & Your Goals

You now may have an idea of the market size along with the initial customer demand or appetite for your service and you are getting excited. The next task is to determine what's most important to you: is it the money, or being home by five p.m.? Is it being in an environment with a peer group, or working alone in the middle of the night in your pajamas?

This ranking is called Maslow's Hierarchy of Needs, and it's the prioritization of your personal desires. It's key to knowing what will guide your choices for the clients you take on (or don't) and how far you are willing to take your business.

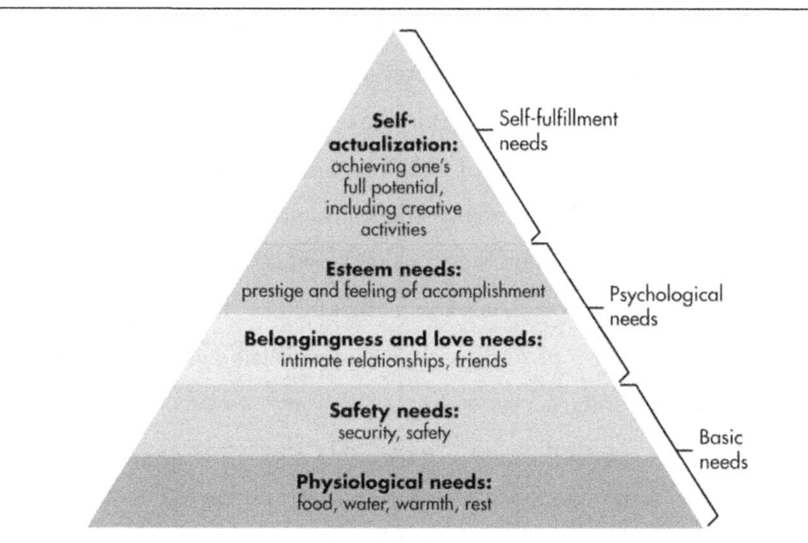

Table 1. Maslow's Hierarchy of Needs

Becky's goal was to have happy, trained puppies and earn a full-time living. This occurred without sacrificing her number one objective, which was well-trained puppies. Others, such as Erika Spry or Laura King, desired extra income while maintaining ultimate flexibility and adherence to a family-centered schedule. Brian Caplovitz and Mike Konesky, on the other hand, were driven by a desire to fill a gap in markets. Revenue and net profits were secondary.

> **Reader time out**: Do you have a service that applies to individuals or companies in multiple sectors? Are you comfortable learning about new markets, products and demographics, and tailoring what you know for a client?

A pattern to replicate for extraordinary growth

Expanding into other industries may be "on the roadmap," and may come from the clients themselves.

Such was the case with Erika Spry. She was perfectly happy consulting to small restaurants when she started receiving referrals to other, small and medium sized business owners for nearly every aspect of business operations, sales and marketing.

"Within a year of starting my business, I had medical laboratories and car companies as clients, along with a few manufacturing companies, non-profits and schools." The projects all revolved around branding, marketing, operational efficiencies, hiring and training.

"I never would have expected it, but today, ten years after I started, I'm really glad," she said. "I'm now a single mom and prefer not to travel, so the expansion of my business—still a sole proprietorship—is perfect for my schedule."

Just because I didn't know about a non-profit business didn't mean I couldn't provide a great website.

Erika Spry

Going cross-industry, one client request at a time

The growth of my company occurred because of client requests. After a year, more than half of my clients asked if I could provide the partner development services for other large, hard to navigate companies, like Amazon, Apple and Google. I expanded outside technology because the clients were focused on increasing sales. Soon, I was working with entertainment, manufacturing, financial services and medical. In under five years, that list had grown to seventeen industries.

Reader time out: Is your company dependent on one industry? If so, consider branching out. It may not be as challenging as you think. What works in one industry might very well work in another—if not in totality, at least in part. This leverages your efforts, accelerating your ability to broaden consulting in a single-industry to multiple industries. The benefit? Lower risk. If one sector is hit hard (think hurricanes and the oil and gas sector) you have spread your risk and revenues are steady.

Spread the risk: Don't rely on a single client

Let's say you have a client that's so large, you could spend your entire career working in a project or consulting capacity and have no reason or need to expand outside this one client. Think IBM, Boeing, Bank of America or even Amazon—organizations with thousands of employees and nearly as many contracts. The range is broad and includes nearly every aspect of business: finance, human resources marketing, sales, integration and more, many with sub-specialties. When you have client that big, the number one goal is to continually mine the organization for future projects. **In other words, you are constantly seeking out new relationships and leveraging your successful projects with additional group**s.

Initially, I used this approach with Microsoft, concentrating a large part of my time during a twelve-month period to knowing as many decision makers in as many different product groups across the primary lines of business as was possible. I was constantly fearful of having my revenue dependent on a single group or decision maker, particularly after reading a few statistics on the subject. According to the career site The Balance (www.thebalance.com) people stay in their jobs less than five years, changing jobs 10-15 times during their career.

After a year, I had contacts in dozens of groups and had a database of several hundred people, enough to create my own organizational chart to diagram the connections, overlaps, decision makers and influencers. As I succeeded in negotiating partner deals with one group, I'd use the project as a reference to get introduced to another product group.

Insider tip: Never rely on one client for more than fifty-percent of your revenue. More conservative thinking takes that down to twenty-percent.

To outsiders (prospects), my established connections were viewed as a huge value-add, because those San Francisco-based entities didn't have the capacity to place a full-time person in Seattle with the exclusive purpose of getting to know Microsoft.

Now to the details of what I did and how I did it. Or in other words, how to extend your base within an organization:

- Understand the group mission/objectives
- Quantify (e.g. get them to reveal) how they are measured for success and/or failure
- Identify if you map into that agenda. If you don't, move on. If you are aligned with the core business objectives, create a strategy to earn a part of that business.
- Earn a place on the budget line item
- After the project is complete, use those references to another associated group.
- Adjunct to this is knowing the other vendors, suppliers, consultants, and contractors associated with this group. That's four groups of people who can all recommend you as a resource or hire you directly.

As you work the day-to-day with your contacts, leverage the growing amount of information you may gather. Specifically, when you are speaking with one group, offer up information about one group that would be helpful to another. You'd be surprised how many individuals are so focused on completing their own tasks that they are ignorant of what other groups are up to. It's not uncommon for a consultant to learn of overlapping initiatives, double efforts or even contradicting objectives. You, the consultant, truly add value when you raise these issues (diplomatically) to the surface. **You are saving the entire company (your client) time and money, and in the process, made yourself an integral and valuable part of the team**.

Ten Consulting Vocations

Working from a home office is ideal. If you're not necessarily interested in being around a staff all the time, consider the following:

1. **Retail Operations Consultant**: consults on creating processes for hiring, business operations, margins, inventory, and loss.
2. **Retail Sales Consultant**; consults on hiring, training, and managing store employees.
3. **Retail Management Consultant**: consults through seminars and internal corporate programs designed to motivate employees, improve performance, and identify high-impact employees.
4. **Retail Design Consultant**: consults on store design, configuration, layout, and colors for the highest output per square footage.

5. **Retail Buying Consultant**: consults on the products to purchase for the highest margins and recommends partners, and distribution channels.
6. **Retail Event Consultant**; consults on in-store and out of store events for promotional purposes with an emphasis on partnering with complimentary organizations.
7. **Outsourced Computer Sales Consultant**: this is very broad with many sub-specialties, from sales techniques, sales operations, sales conflict management, sales recruiting and more. A growing market is training sales professionals with non-US-based customers (e.g. those who work with and travel to other parts of the world). Did you know that consultants exist for sales training specifically for sales reps who travel to each major continent, and within that, specific territories? If you've spent time in Argentina, for example, and know the language, customers, etc., you could set up a service exclusively for manufacturers who have products sourced from this county.
8. **Résumé Consultant**: consults individuals, or corporate clients on the best résumé for a specific profession.
9. **Dog Training Consultant**: consults with individuals, groups or corporate pet stores to provide training for a specific breed, size or age of dogs.
10. **Partner Management Consultant:** consults to companies who desire improved partner-created revenue.

Action Items: Stage 2

- ✓ Identify an existing market for your services. If you can't find one that maps to your priorities, conduct an exercise where you can "create" a market that will pay for your knowledge.
- ✓ Conduct all the market research you can. If possible, reach out to industry experts or research articles and the media. This will tell you where "the market" stands on your potential service offering.
- ✓ Validate your potential service offering with prospective clients.
- ✓ When calling prospective clients (or referral partners), don't be shy about asking if your fees are in line with expectations.
- ✓ Determine the level of consumer demand as critical, important, or just interesting.
- ✓ Align your schedule and offering with your personal desires or needs. This ensures your short-term revenue objectives are met as well as your long-term goals for the company.
- ✓ Specialize in an area of the niche to prove your services and gain references.

This was a lot of information and work, wasn't it? It will pay off, trust me. And I expect you may have a bit of fear and trepidation about getting on the phone.

Breathe. That's normal. As Erika Spry said, "I could always do the work, but it terrified me to stick my hand out, introduce myself and talk about what I do for a living. I had to force myself to do it. After a while, it became second nature. Now, some of my greatest referrals come from the unlikeliest sources (think my nail lady), but everyone knows someone with a business who needs help, and that person can be me."

Everyone you come in contact knows a person who runs or owns a business. Make sure they know what you do, so when the time comes, you get the call, not someone else.

As you move to Stage 3, repeat that to yourself, and add: "That person can be me."

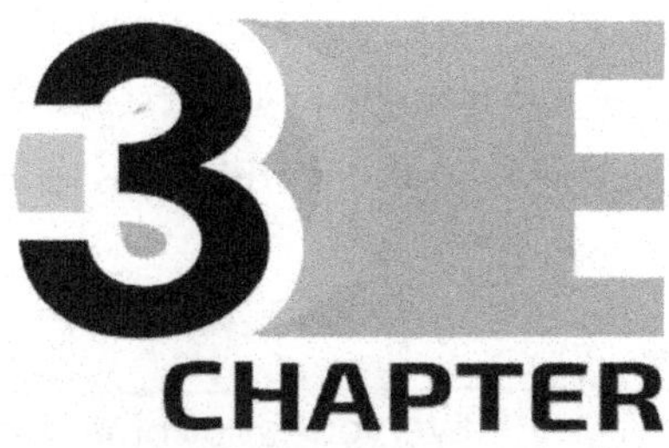

You never lose a dream. It just incubates as a hobby.

Larry Page, CEO, Alphabet (parent company of Google)

Chapter Three: Defining Your Services

People understand Chinese menus, but that's not always the best way to offer services. This approach minimizes the value of the service and ensures that you are continually in the job-seeking mode. This chapter focuses on the art of constructing and balancing long-term, project-based services with short, high-profit spot projects.

Defining Your Offering

Creating a (virtual or physical) one-page offering sheet is a disciplined approach to gaining clarity about your service offerings. Six questions must be answered:

1. What service am I offering?
2. Why does this make sense? And to whom does it make sense?
3. How am I different from the existing options and/or alternatives?
4. What can you expect as a result of my service offerings?

5. What is the price of my offerings?
6. What guarantee will I offer along with my services?

An **elevator pitch** is a brief, persuasive speech that you use to spark interest in what your organization provides. You can also use it to create aa in awareness for a project, idea, or product – or in yourself. A **good elevator pitch** should last no longer than a short **elevator** ride of 20 to 30 seconds, hence the name.

I'll give you two different elevator pitches that are being used anywhere (rarely in the elevator). When you are starting out, it's helpful to write down what you intend to say, and then time yourself. If you can keep it to 30 seconds, you are on the right path.

Automotive Consultant

I'm Bryan Kelley, and I own and operate an automotive repair center servicing the greater Eastside of Seattle. I also train repair technicians from around the region who are interested in keeping up with the latest developments in automotive repair. Our company is known for fast, reliable service at an affordable price, where customer loyalty and satisfaction come first. We'll tell you what's critical to your safety, what needs to be done in the near future and what you can do yourself. We bill hourly and by the project, and tell you if it's going to change before we do the job.

In Bryan's elevator pitch, he reveals the pricing structure near the end, right after the client benefit of benefits.

Organizational Consultant

I'm Laura King, and I'm a professional organizational expert who provides customized services based on your home, office, or life needs. If you've outgrown your existing space, added a new child to the family, or need to reconfigure your office environment for maximum productivity, I'm your resource for structuring and changing your environment. Most consultants either offer an expensive closet system, squish in a tremendous number of cubicles or do little more than clean a cluttered room. My approach is to redefine your space, organize the items in a way that makes sense to you, and then maximize your living environment. I've found that my clients can reorganize an entire house for less than the cost of a single closet system. And after I get done, that system is not even required!

Play around with your own version of the elevator pitch, and try it out on a few associates or potential clients. It needs to be used to be refined. It's also the start of your client pipeline. Once you have it down, and you are receiving positive responses, it's time to consider the other forms of external communication.

Your On-Line Presence

If you are doing this "on the side," while keeping a full-time job, you may not want a web presence at all, or at least one that references you by name. Referrals and word of mouth may be the only communication vehicle you require. The salient point is this: keep it simple and keep it appropriate for your budget, time constraints and requirement.

A great website doesn't necessarily translate into a lot of projects or improved profitability.

On the other hand, if this is your full-time job, a website is the default choice for most businesses, and fortunately, websites are easy and inexpensive to construct (just ask Erika Spry). A website will suffice for some businesses, but not all. Consider what a website accomplishes:

1. Validates your presence
2. A picture of you, an address, and an overview of services
3. Provides the basic details of your business along with references
4. Customers, quotes, success stories and an inquiry form to filter prospective clients
5. Highlights competitive advantages
6. Prospective clients read, review, and compare your services with others, reducing wasted time
7. Identifies business process
8. Explains how you like to do business ensures that your working philosophy is aligned with a prospective client before they place a call to you
9. Builds referral networking
10. Links with other partners in complimentary business and you them, creating a nice referral network at no cost

Free website tools abound, and many will create and host a basic website for free. Modest upgrades to the site, such as the inclusion of 2-5 email accounts with your company name and other services are usually offered at modest prices, such as $5/month, and become more expensive as you add levels of sophistication.

Your First Meeting

Whether it takes place at the counter of a coffee shop, or in an executive office suite, your pitch must be professional and concise, and fulfill a specific set of meeting objectives. You are not only pitching the individual, you are assessing that person on the merits of what type of client they might turn out to be. Success in business is more about the client you don't accept, than the client you do. The point is that a single bad experience in business might cost more in terms of personnel, reputation, and money than ten great clients will earn you.

Success in business is more about the client you don't accept than the client you do.

Mike Konesky feels that the most compelling sales tool is a consultant's **level of confidence**, whether it's the first meeting or the closing discussion.

"Even without a pitch or a single sales tool, I was confident that I knew the business part of the job and could make the sale," said Konesky. For Konesky, his confidence was derived from being exposed to all aspects of the consulting business from actual estimating, planning, and delivery to oversight and management. During his initial meeting with his first prospective client, he had the confidence to express that he knew how to do the job, but also how well-managed consulting companies operated. With front and back office tasks understood and under his belt, the confidence came naturally.

In addition to the attitude of confidence, animal consultant Becky Bishop believes her two bestselling tools are her ability to **understand the competitive offerings** and also, her aptitude to **talk about her differentiation**.

Becky confides that her most enlightening competitive research was done when she showed up at a local dog training school. She saw so many mistakes, she learned what not to do and say. She validated her competitive advantage was based in her dramatically different approach. Armed with first-hand knowledge, she could back-up her hypothesis of training differentiation with real comparative points, along with the pros and cons of each style of training.

Your confidence, competitive advantage and ability to communicate your skills are going to result in a first meeting or phone call with a potential client. Your task is to determine if they are the right type of client for you to accept, and if the project itself has a high chance for success. Remember, when you are starting out, every client needs to be referenceable. The first and most important step is to gather as much information about the project as possible.

Create a prospect project sheet and answer as many question as you can, then follow up with a call or meeting to gather the remainder of the information.

Prospect Qualification Sheet

✓ What is the line of business, product, or service required?

  - Dog training, organizational help, software application

- ✓ Does this fit with your service offerings?
- ✓ What is the scope of the project?
    - One dog or twenty, one room or five plus and office, a single application or one to support thousands of people
- ✓ Is this person the decision maker?
    - Does he/she rely on the input of others? Does the project have a dependency on others or different groups?
- ✓ Does the individual or company have a specific milestone, timeframe, or event it is trying to meet?
- ✓ Is the project budgeted?
- ✓ If not, what's the timeframe for a decision, and what's the process?
    - Does the homeowner need to talk with a spouse? Must the software application proposal go before a committee that meets once a quarter?
- ✓ What does the prospective client expect of you? Is it realistic for the outlined and budgeted?"
- ✓ Do you *like* the person with whom you are talking, and what is your *gut* telling you?
    - Are the answers clear cut, readily available or is it taking a lot of time, effort and energy to get the simple questions answered? These are call signals towards or against taking on the project.

A good rule of thumb is that the greater the complexity and cost of the project, the greater the upfront time and effort required to gather the data. Therefore, one or more calls with the prospective client will be necessary to get the data.

If you have gathered enough information to justify a second meeting, (e.g. you have determined that this is a project you'd like to take on, the expectations match with your skills, the price is generally acceptable to both parties), then you set your first in-person meeting to discuss the details.

Project Details Agenda

- ✓ Reviewing the client's objectives, products, and services
- ✓ Providing a deeper understanding of your consulting offerings (via presentation)
- ✓ Engaging in a discussion about potential working scenarios
- ✓ Cost and timeframes for deliverables
- ✓ Confirming the next steps

You may want to create an agenda with these five elements, and send it forward via email prior to the meeting. That way, your potential client validates and agrees upon the topics, and is prepared to commit to the project.

I'll give you an example of a woman who uses both checklists to scope out the project in the first phone call and the second checklist for either a call or in-person meeting.

A friend of mine was the coordinator for the local Entrepreneur's Organization (EO), (www.eonetwork.org), formerly known as the Young Entrepreneur's Organization. In this role, she worked with dozens of CEOs of companies with revenue between $1 million and $5 million.

During her time as coordinator, she often became friends with the CEOs, and gradually learned enough about the business needs of the EO executives to provide unsolicited feedback. It wasn't long until her comments proved helpful, and the CEOs wanted to hire her for internal reviews of their own businesses.

Unknown to her at the time, the vocation had a title: Life Coach. Already armed with her bachelor's degree in psychology, she added several more professional certifications as she started her consulting business. **Her revenue per month tripled from about $2,000 a month to nearly $6,500**. In addition to serving small businesses in her region, she has added individual clients that include top-ranking executives from Alaska Airlines and Microsoft. Within two years, she was making $250,000 per year, about half of her work conducted at the client site, the other half from the comfort of her home.

When I asked for details on her sales pitch, she admitted to using a list of questions over the phone as a means of qualifying prospective clients. She'd never used a physical or visual presentation.

"This is a "people-business,"" she explained. "And I can't work with someone who isn't willing to be open and honest about their issues, nor can I help a person or organization that can't take serious feedback." She didn't need to be sitting in front of a person to quality a prospective client. As such, **she includes a set of qualifying questions**

she asks throughout the interview to help her determine whether a working relationship will be positive.

"I am a one-person shop, so every client has to be a reference for me," she explained. "If I sense resistance to my approach at any time during the calls or the in-person meeting, then I tend to not take on the project. It's not an issue of the money, it's the opportunity cost of having an engagement that isn't successful, and both parties are unhappy."

Nothing says as much about your business as a referral from another well-respected professional who knows what you can achieve. As my friend in sales found, she received referrals from her former employers and was offered an open door to work hourly, from home, on a consulting basis, at her discretion.

Always provide value...on every call, email or other interaction. Become a source your customer or partner can depend upon.

This is an over-used phrase, yet it's misunderstood and rarely employed by new consultants. In blunt terms, providing value means you are educating or giving knowledge away for free. This doesn't mean you must spend ten hours providing a plan and turning it over at the first meeting. Rather, the intent is to show you have put thought and consideration into the client's goals, and you can offer a few suggestions as to how you can address their needs.

The professional life coach invariably brings up a half-dozen solutions to the prospect's identifiable problems during the first meeting.

"As a result, the individual can walk out of the meeting feeling like they've learned something and employ my comments immediately," she says. This, in turn, increases her prospect's understanding of the value of what she's offering, and is even more willing to pay her hourly rates.

"Ultimately, I want them hungry for more," she continued. "Once the client has signed the contract, I evolve the client from once or twice a month to weekly sessions. And it all starts by adding value up front."

My motto has always been to provide at least one thing of value to anyone I talk with, partners or clients alike. If I'm pitching a story for a client to an editor, I'll also give one or two ideas completely unrelated to my primary goal. By doing so, I move from being a one-sided marketing and business development professional to a trusted source of interesting ideas.

Leave Behind Information

Fewer and fewer companies provide written marketing materials at all, unless it's a product specification. I did away with printed collateral years ago. Only for special client presentations do I print out physical copies for on-site handouts, which enables participants to take notes. The downside is that someone will invariably flip through the presentation and this can be distracting.

Still, it's better to have a renegade participant than disappoint the prospective client by looking unprepared or cheap.

Over the years, I've tried a variety of leave-behinds. One of the most effective has been business-card USB and SD disks that I purchased up at a retail office supply company. I loaded my presentation and other brochure materials in PDF format and handed them out at the end of the meeting. This was much handier and less expensive than carrying around bags of paper and business cards.

Statistically, it costs a business between five and six times more to attract a new customer than keep an existing one.[1] And while only one out of 25 customers will express dissatisfaction,[2] happy customers tell four to five others of their positive experience. Contrast this to the single dissatisfied customer that tells nine to twelve people they had a bad experience![3]

Offering a Guarantee

Consider this. You have the elevator pitch, a web site and USB card to hand out when the time is right. So, what if a person is interested, and naturally asks about a guarantee. You stop and give them a blank stare.

Guarantee? As in, money back guarantee? Yep, that's why we are covering it right now, because it will surely come up, and you need to be prepared.

---

[1] Extreme Management, Mark Stevens.

[2] Customer Intimacy, Fred Wiersema.

Guarantees are a hot-button topic, sure to set off a philosophical divide of biblical proportions. Proponents believe that offering a guarantee establishes a foundation of trust and commitment stemming from the consultant's willingness to do anything to "get it right." Further, **the words "satisfaction guaranteed" adds another level of comfort to the engagement**. The counterpoint of this thinking is the inherent risk a consultant takes if the client can't be satisfied, no matter the outcome, and money will be returned, even if it was the client that erred.

So, where is the dividing line between risk on the part of the consultant and comfort for the client?

Some consultants offer a very strongly worded guarantee, while others offer none at all. You, the enterprising small business owner, want satisfied clients who will refer you a lot of business. If you can, it's best to give a guarantee of sorts, up front, at least for the first few clients, until your reputation is established.

Take attorney David Johnstone, who practices law at his Washington, D.C. office by day, and edits manuscripts from novices and New York Times bestselling authors alike at night. He found that he loved editing in college, and had a proficiency and interest beyond making a few hundred bucks.

Once he began practicing law, he realized that his 401K plan might not weather the economic ups and down's, so he decided to allocate any extra money earned through editing for his retirement. He formally formed Johnstone Editorial Consulting, and since opening his doors, as edited more than 120 books.

David's guarantee is not as simple as complete happiness or unhappiness with a project.

"It's a mixture of the client liking my suggestions and comments, as well as the time in which the project was completed," said David. Since he is paid over the course of a project, it's less risky for the client. Yet, since the last payment is usually the largest, **David does his best to ensure satisfaction along the way, not sending the final invoice until the client signs off on the project and is fully satisfied.**

"Of course, I could always get stiffed after I've delivered the manuscript, but that's never happened." Since it pays (a lot) to keep your clients happy, identify your policy up front, either on your website as a competitive differentiation, or in your materials. Of course, communicating your policy should be stated verbally during the initial conversations as a sales tool. If it hasn't come up prior to signing the contract, don't be shy about reinforcing your position. It's much better to have the discussion before the project has begun (even at the risk of losing the contract) than what will happen if the engagement ends poorly. The last outcome you want or need is a dissatisfied client going on the Internet and criticizing your work.

Mike Konesky of Northwest Results insists on 100% referenceable clients, just like the life coach. To ensure this happens, he's had to go above and beyond what was contractually scoped to ensure a satisfied client.

"I make sure to provide a status at least weekly, including budget and any issues have arisen." This is how he and the client address any concerns before a problem becomes a real detriment. "**A surprised client is an unhappy client**. I don't like surprises, nor do my clients."

Even so, Konesky has had a few unhappy clients in the past. In those cases, he came to a reasonable solution. If the client has increased the original scope of work, or if the client didn't deliver as expected, Konesky expects the client to bear the cost of the change. "And in the rare situation where a client was still dissatisfied, with what I, or my team have delivered, I've had to eat those costs." Period.

Caryn Leifer, CEO of Leifer Legal Nurse Consulting, (www.cleifer.com), out of Mt. Laurel, NJ, offers a 100% guarantee, and this is stated at the top of her website. Consultants in her niche review, analyze, screen, and compare medical documents, as well as assist and attend depositions, trials, and arbitration and mediation hearings. The stakes are high. Caryn's clients are the attorneys, who rely on an expert opinion well before the case proceeds to litigation.

In that environment, she must offer a guarantee with a caveat. As a Legal Nurse Consultant, the offer is as stated: "If, for any reason, you are not entirely satisfied with our work product…" The only stipulation is that her firm be notified within ten business days so she can revise the work product to meet the client's specifications to ensure satisfaction.

Legal or Landscaping, Customer Satisfaction Matters

Consider a completely different business, but just as expensive: landscape consulting. Our lawn was being landscaped, and we had sod placed on roughly an acre. Surrounding this was natural landscape, augmented with sprinklers and a variety of indigenous plants. It was about thirty percent of the landscaping bill, but we figured it was worth it, so wrote the check and had instant, lush green grass.

For two weeks.

The grass died first. Then the rose bushes contracted fungus, and our contractor pointed the finger at the landscape consultant, who had specified the materials and the lawn systems and had overseen the entire project. Part of his management fee was to ensure that the right pieces were installed.

To the contractor's delight, the consultant had to take full responsibility. The land had previously been horse pasture, and it was full of a type of grub that destroyed most sod products. It hadn't been tested before he specified the sod product. Further, the sprinklers around the ornamental bushes were placed above ground, splashing all types of fungus from the ground onto the plants, killing them. His cost to remedy the situation was about $15,000, and as I recall, he just about had a heart attack (he was a sole proprietor and we were his fourth or fifth job).

But my dissatisfaction at having a destroyed lawn with a wedding reception just weeks away pushed him to make things right. In the end, the landscape consultant worked out a deal with the contractor to spread out the immediate cost of the big machinery and labor of installing the new sod. He also got lucky with the sod supplier, who offered to take a portion of responsibility for not offering to test and verify the quality and grade of the soil before selling and installing the sod.

The landscape consultant's guarantee was that the customer would be happy with the outcome. It wasn't in writing, but it was a part of his business DNA. Instead of vilifying him to prospects, I recommended him as an honest guy who made a mistake, but provided great work and great conflict resolution skills. **After all, it was a learning experience for him, and as a consultant myself, I had empathy and appreciation for how he handled himself.** Little did I know that I would soon have the chance to make amends to my own client after a failed engagement.

Admit, Acknowledge, Make it Right

About four years after starting BMG, the CEO of a large, privately held staffing company that made the Forbes Inc. 500 fastest growing companies of the year, contacted me about creating a business document to be used in discussions with a strategic partner. My own project plate was full, but one of my senior business development consultants had extra time in his schedule to take on a new project. The CEO was comfortable in my decision to assign the project to this consultant if I guaranteed my oversight.

For thirty days, my employee worked with the client team, interviewing management, researching, and presenting options to me for regular input. I'd also read the corporate materials and attended the project kick-off meeting and weekly update sessions, so felt I had a good grasp on the program goal. When it came time for me to review the business plan, I disagreed with many of the conclusions and recommendations.

We were several days away from delivering the draft document when I recommended dramatic changes without giving due consideration to the fact he was the consultant with more working knowledge of the program, the people, and the inputs that derived the conclusions.

By now, you can see where this is headed. The chief executive hated the document so much he came home from his vacation several days early, believing he'd have to rewrite entire thing himself over the weekend. That wasn't all. He gave me the single worst dressing-down of my career. Beyond telling me the document showed how out of touch we were with his organization, the people, and the direction, my employee's conclusions were baseless. He swore that if the partnership were to go south, he would not only demand that we return the money that had already been paid, but also tell everyone he knew about his bad experience.

The phrase "falling on my sword" was invented for this type of situation, and I eagerly used it. Like my landscape consultant, I began by taking full responsibility, owning the document as opposed to blaming it on a subordinate. Part and parcel to this action was admitting my error in judgment to my employee, apologizing for not listening or trusting his work product.

My promise to make it right to the client was followed up by my guarantee for his satisfaction: I'd return the money that had been paid in full, about $15,000 (ironically the amount of the landscaper's error), that day. But what I really wanted was the opportunity to set it right. I told him about the original document and requested he give it a read-through.

Thankfully, this chief executive appreciated I owned up to my mistakes.

"The key to success," he told me, "was that you admitted you didn't know it all." He ended by telling me that the hardest lesson to learn is how to admit a wrong, take ownership, and make it right. "Too few small business owners learn it fast enough, and by the time they do, their business is already in trouble."

Prior to this experience, the necessity for a guarantee hadn't arisen. Afterward, I provided the policy up front as a selling tool. While I have no data proving that it aided in gaining client engagements, it certainly seemed to have a positive impact. (For an epilogue, he liked the first document and used it, thereby not requiring me to return the money).

Bryan Kelley had a similar experience, but in his case, "one of my technicians was shorting all the customers." The technician (the person who works on the cars), was making shortcuts. "It was little things," Bryan explained, "but could cause serious issues to the car. For example, on an oil change, if the technician doesn't clean down to the steel, it will work for about thirty days and then start to leak. The customer would leave and the car worked fine, but thirty days later, they'd be back in." Kelley noticed a trend within about forty-five days. "Leaking oil is a one thing, but it was indicative of a pattern which could absolutely kill a car."

Bryan confronted the technician who didn't want to stay and make it right, because fixing the cars would to be done without pay. Bryan had a choice: to call all the customers who this technician had worked on the cars in question, or do nothing.

"I called every one of them," he recounted. "About eighty in total." He asked each owner to bring in their car to be checked for free, and if any work was required, it too, would be done at no cost. At first, he didn't want to reveal why, and was promptly accused of not being trustworthy. "By the fifth call, I was upfront. I explained we found issues with a technician who was no longer employed, and we wanted to guarantee our work was quality." The response was dramatically different. **"Those first five customers came in, we fixed the cars and we never saw them again. The other seventy-five or so have been loyal and keep coming back."**

Erika Spry has had her share of failures, large and small.

"I have carbon copied someone when it should have been blind copied, and made bad judgement calls which made me want to crawl under a rock and never come out." Her solution? "Take responsibility, accept it and make it right one hundred percent of the time. Once you do that, the client has no more anger, and wants to fix the problem and move on."

Erika's motto of "making it right," translates to "doing whatever it takes to make the client happy." While she doesn't have it in writing, it's her word, and her reputation. That's enough.

Certain instances do arise, however, where a guarantee can't be maintained (even in writing) due to the onus on the client once the initial project is complete.

When Guarantees aren't possible: Client Responsibility

This is the case with Becky's animal training. Becky's likens her business to an auto mechanic that gets your car back to running well.

You *still* must maintain it, and if you don't, it will run poorly again and it's not the mechanics fault. If her clients don't maintain the training, the behavior will slide. That's not the dog trainer's fault, it's the owners.

When it comes to guarantees, "You cannot guarantee dog training," she maintains. In fact, she goes so far as to tell people if a trainer takes your dog and guarantees the training will stick, think twice. This increases her reliance on her instinct and ability to accept clients she believes share the same philosophy of dog training.

Lucky for Becky, in the years she has been providing animal consulting, she's never had a client call back and tell her, "The dog isn't really trained, and it's your fault. They always know where the fault lies."

Guarantees should be considered as a means to help promote the initial sale, as well as continue good relations with clients if a project doesn't meet expectations. Over the years, service providers who are small businesses have gotten creative in offering all types of guarantees that don't require the return of money. Check out a few of the guarantee options available to consultants across five vocations.

Consulting Guarantee Options to Consider

- ✓ **Staffing**: Full return-refund if an individual placed doesn't work out in 30 days. Scaled or pro-rated if it's 60–90 days. Staffing firm Radnor Consulting (www.radnorconsulting.com) offers a 100-day full money-back guarantee.
- ✓ **Web and Internet consulting**: Inspire Consulting (www.inspire-consulting.com) helps businesses grow revenue through website

development. Inspire offers a satisfaction-guarantee policy, proudly stating that it will continue working until the customer is completely satisfied.

- ✓ **General consulting**: Offer a credit to the company for a future product if an engagement doesn't meet customer expectations.
- ✓ **Small project consulting**, such as design, space organization, or even audio-equipment consulting: The 100% satisfaction guarantee means that a room or space of equivalent size will be given the same service at no charge.
- ✓ **Military or technical consulting**: Offer a free evaluation of a separate project that the client requires, knowing that this alone might turn into yet another engagement.

Ten Consulting Vocations

Worked in education, for libraries or non-profits? Turn this into a consulting practice by becoming a:

1. **Non-Profit Consultant**: consults to non-profits about one subject or can consult to one non-profit, focusing on all facets of the organization.
2. **Corporate Library Consultant**: consults to mid and large size organizations on defining, creating, structuring, acquiring, and improving corporate libraries.
3. **Grant Consultant**: consults to non-profits (or picks a type) to find the best type of grant and manages it to completion.

4. **Non-profit Partnership Consultant**: consults corporations on how to establish an internal non-profit group or foundation.
5. **School Procurement Consultant**: consults to businesses seeking to buy into a publicly funded school, counseling clients on the processes, procedures, documents and dependencies.
6. **Partner Development Consulting**: consults clients on identifying, pitching, creating and implementing revenue producing partnerships.
7. **Life Coach Consultant**: consults with individual or corporate clients on improving goal attainment through improved interpersonal, leadership, or management coaching.
8. **Legal Nurse Consultant**: consults to lawyers or corporations as an expert witness, researcher or secondary review opinion in litigation.
9. **Internet Consultant**: consults on any Internet related specialty areas, from web design, ecommerce strategies, sales, email, or marketing effectiveness.
10. **Staffing Consultant**: consults to corporate clients on hiring practices, placing individuals, or improving retention.

Action Items: Stage 3

- ✓ Answer the five questions related to defining your company.
- ✓ Prepare the written elevator pitch that even your grandmother will understand.

- ✓ Establish a website presence, and/or create and customize a physical presentation as necessary.
- ✓ Pre-qualify your prospective clients before the meeting, and finish during the in-person session.
- ✓ Always provide free value during the meeting and every interaction thereafter.
- ✓ When a failure does occur, take immediate and full responsibility. Do all within your power to "make it right," to ensure customer satisfaction.
- ✓ Consider the use of a guarantee.

Wow. You've come a long way. You have your goals set, validated the target market for your services, created the materials required, set up your work space and are ready to go. You might have already had and completed your first client project. Good job! Now you're prepared to go full force and selling a lot of clients, right?

Take a pause long enough to read Chapter four, which zeroes in on making money and realizing projects, and yes, there is a difference. Revenue is part of the equation, but as Bryan Kelley learned, profits are another.

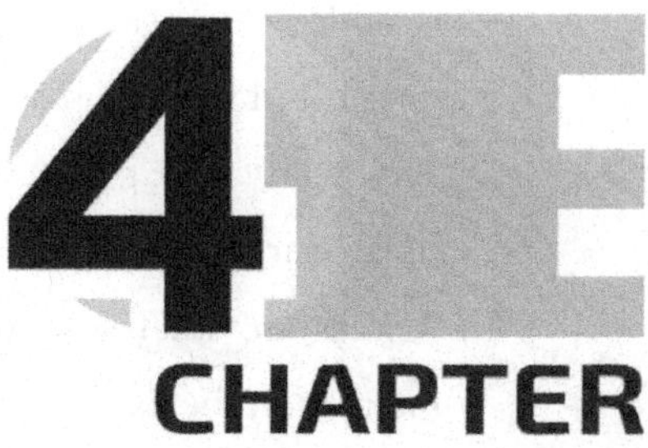

Selling is a natural skill. You develop it as a child. It's called persuasion.

Jeffrey Gitomer

Chapter Four: Making Money aka Getting Paid

Invariably, the subject that causes that most angst among new consultants involves setting the price. The question: "Why are *you* worth that?" is challenging for most people to answer. It's why athletes and other celebrities have third-party representation who objectively and shamelessly list every single attribute contributing to value, along with a corresponding dollar amount.

Establishing value starts with the first conversation. As you describe your services, you set the expectations about fees by what you say, how you say it, and connect the value to the outcomes. The prospective client ascertains whether the service is affordable or not (agreeing, smiling head-nodding). Failing to provide the groundwork for what you will eventually charge annoys the prospect and unnecessarily drags on (or entirely hinders) the pricing conversation.

Some consulting services require a review of the project or situation. For Laura's organizing service, she must see the space, room, or office to give a realistic bid. Housecleaning, moving, and mowing services offer the same approach, as does business and partner development consulting.

Scoping the Work

Mike Konesky uses the word Assessment for his free, two-day session to understand the project and create his own summary "assessment" of what's required. (If the prospect is local, it's free. When the prospective client is out of town, prospects pay for travel and lodging). This is the basis for a **Statement of Work (SOW)**, a formal document that **lists the details of the project, dependencies, costs** etc. It's common for consulting firms to charge between $1-2,000 for the assessment alone, and it's non-refundable. Because Mike's assessment and SOW is free, the prospects are understandably thrilled.

"Two days gives me enough time to understand the business issues, but also to get the prospect invested in me as a consultant," Mike maintains. The prospect is less inclined to spend two full days with another consultant who is going to charge money to get educated.

Even the life coach gives a one-time, free of charge hourly "consultation," to prospects; and you will read about others in this chapter.

If your project is more than a thousand dollars, it may require scoping out the work and providing a document, free of charge, to win the business.

Establishing value starts with the first conversation

Hourly versus Project

As a rule of thumb, consulting is almost always more profitable when done by project, as it allows the fee to be attached to the value of the consulting project as opposed to a fixed hourly rate.

Unfortunately, a common misperception associated with project fees is that the price is being unnecessarily padded.

One way to address this concern is to include a "**not-to-exceed**" clause with details. This identifies that **the project fee is fixed based upon the details in the contract and won't go over budget**. This gives the client peace of mind, even if the price is a little higher. Of course, if the client decides to change the project (add two more dogs to the training, or two more individuals for executive coaching instead of one that was contracted), a change in the documentation is required.[3]

Konesky applies the same type of pricing structure, although he's in technology consulting. He offers a mix of fixed hourly rate, a project based with a flat fee and an adjustable hourly rate. Each is explained in a paragraph format that's easy to understand.

---

[3] Depending on your industry, amending the contract can be a simple one-page document, with various titles: Work order change, Statement of Work Addendum, Scope change addendum etc. Regardless of the title or name, the original details, and the new client-requested items must be included, the document dated and signed by both parties.

Let's return to Becky Bishop and her animal consulting business. I truly love her example, because of her commonsense approach to pricing. As her revenue shows, her enthusiasm and results quickly catapulted her hourly into thousands of dollars per year in income.

Back in 1995, Becky charged her first client, a family with one puppy, $35.00 for 1.5 hours. She recalls that she was so excited and had so much passion, she ended up staying three hours, until the family hinted it was dinner time and she should scoot. But the family loved the results, and Becky received many referrals from that first client.

She continued to use her hourly rate during the first year, working one-on-one with clients, usually at their homes. During the first few months, she cleared $3,000.00. The following year, she started offering short-term boarding and training at her home for difficult puppies, and her business tripled. This wasn't hourly billing, but daily, weekly, or other flat fee rates. This allowed her to have a stable income while continuing her hourly rates that, by then, had increased.

Today, Becky is proud to report that her firm is incorporated and pays her a salary of $60,000.00 a year while the corporation grosses over $350,000.00 a year.

"I guess it's fair to say that I now work for me," she says. And a person whose grand ambition was to successfully train her own puppy created this profitable business.

Linking Commissions with Revenue

Clients love a consultant who participates in helping grow revenue and receives payment based on results. In this structure, the consultant shares in the risk and return and is perceived to work harder than if the fee were unlinked. If your efforts directly relate to the sales of a product, then you should consider this option. (What that means is if you are working in the marketing, partnership, business development or sales aspects of the business, it's possible you have the option for commissions on sales).

Generally, commissions range from one percent to twenty percent—again, depending on the industry, product etc. The weighty factor is the risk taken by the consultant upfront in return for a greater payout on the back end.

Within the contract language, you will want to ensure you are using the right terminology to describe the ways you will get paid, as it's the terms of when the commissions are paid out that usually trips up the structure.

Before a consultant offers this as an option, five questions should be asked and answered:

Commission Evaluation Guidelines

1. Will the engagement affect all company revenue or any specific product(s)?
2. How is the revenue tracked and reported? (e.g., daily, monthly, quarterly)
3. When are payments received? (Retail can be up to six months; Internet sales are immediate).
4. When would the commissions be paid? (e.g., bi-weekly, monthly, quarterly)

5. How long is the tail? In other words, the consultant may have worked on client activities that result in a sale after the engagement formally ends.

The consultant will normally be paid on sales for a period, say, six months after project completion. This is known as a tail. Some tails are six months but I'm aware of tails up to 18-24 months if the sales cycles are long, and the consultant has dramatically impacted the revenue.

Of course, exceptions to this rule exist. Consider public relations consultants or agencies. You won't find a single firm or PR professional who will link payment to actual press coverage. The argument here is that the agency doesn't control the final placement of an article; that's done by the magazine or paper. A national emergency could arise, a better story could appear, the organization could receive fewer ad pages, or a whole host of items preventing a story from appearing. Yet, the agency has done all the work, and perhaps even received a commitment from the editor to run the story.

This isn't to say a PR consultant couldn't include a bonus fee if a certain number of stories appeared.

In the case of a consultant working in the retail area, the ability to track impact on sales would depend on the engagement. The burden of tracking and managing the outcomes might not be worth the hassle, so a consultant may elect to use a retainer or project fee.

Other Back-End Fees

Commissions on sales is only one type of back-end fees a consultant can receive at the end of a project. Payment can come in the form of stock in a company, but if the company doesn't provide stock, cash, even a lump sum could be provided if a client is purchased, or has some other major event that might affect the value. If your consulting engagement materially affects any of these significant events, you will want to include back-end fees to be appropriately compensated.

When you are including these fees within your contract, the legal language must contemplate every possible scenario of payment that your client might receive. For instance, if your efforts improve the revenue of a product line, and then an outside entity purchases the product line in an all-stock swap, your consulting contract must include language detailing your payment in an all-stock deal. Failure to do this sets up a tense discussion with the client's attorneys about how to provide you with stock, or the cash-equivalent compensation.

A sister subject to this is who, exactly, will pay you in case of an acquisition.

"The client, of course!" would be the logical answer. Not so, I must reply. Firms acquiring a product line or the entire company typically pay all fees. This is one of the reasons why an acquiring company will go through a process called "due diligence." When it applies to a product, the phrase is "product or technical due diligence." As this is occurring, the "financial due diligence," will be happening in parallel. This requires disclosure of all financial obligations associated with the entity in question. This is considered the liability, and will be included in the list of outstanding debts/liabilities. Acquiring entities can drag out payments of liabilities for an extended period, something you don't want to happen.

Account for this scenario by including language in your consulting contract that stipulates payment within thirty days of a closed transaction. This will ensure that you are paid at the same time all the other creditors will be paid.

My fifth client had a great technology for mobile purchasing. I pitched the technology to Amazon, IBM and Microsoft, and a bidding frenzy began. 45 days later, Amazon purchased the company. I eagerly awaited my back-end commission of the sale price, approximately a quarter of a million dollars. When I got a call asking me if I wanted my check for twenty thousand wired or a check sent, I blanked. **I didn't account for a mix transaction of cash and stock and it cost me $230K.** The consulting contract only covered cash acquisitions, not a mix. As a result, I got absolutely nothing for the stock value of the deal. Luckily, my client did give me all the credit in the press, and that helped attract a lot of future business. Still, it took a long time to make up the money I left on the table.

Trading for Services

If your business is producing enough revenue to support your lifestyle, it might be useful to consider trading services in the right situations. My neighbor traded engineering consulting services for new granite countertops for his kitchen. His fees were about $3,000, and the retail cost of the countertops was going to be approximately $6,000. He came out ahead $3,000.

As a side note, trading is useful, but does have tax implications. The IRS (http://www.irs.gov/taxtopics/tc420.html) defines a trade as a barter. This occurs when you are exchanging goods or services without exchanging money. In fact, the value of this barter, or trade, as it is more commonly known, is taxable in the year it's performed. Generally, this income is reported on a 1040 form, Schedule C.

A trade for services might also be useful when one or both companies value a service of the other so much that the fee will be waived entirely. Lastly, in very rare situations, it's the time of the person(s) or entity involved that's impossible to get, no matter how much was paid.

In my own situation, the executives of movie studio Warp Films (www.warpllc.com) based in Los Angeles contacted me for partner consulting work. The team required a complete partner strategy for a new subsidiary, and someone to approach potential partners and sponsors for movie, Internet, and mobile properties. The fee offered was large, and the opportunity fantastic.

I had other ideas. I had written a young adult fiction novel that my agent had been trying to place with mainstream publishers. The rejections were polite and vague, a "No," without telling me why. "Almost there," was a common refrain, but no further guidance was given. After a year of this, I was prepared to trade a good size project to get real feedback.

After completing the first project for Warp, I pitched producer Lucas Foster about a trade for the next program. He was the producer behind Mr. and Mrs. Smith, Law Abiding Citizen, Jumper and many others. Combined, his movies had produced revenue of over three billion dollars at the box office. My pitch was straightforward: I'd work for thirty days without a fee if he would read one of my properties (that's what a book or manuscript is called in the film world), and he'd provide me with feedback and direction. If he liked it, he'd further it along to the most appropriate media channel.

To be frank, he wasn't thrilled. The scarcest commodity in his world is time, and the lack thereof. He was more interested in cutting a check than spending hours reading what he guessed was going to be a less-than-stellar property from a first-time fiction author. I had to entice him by pointing out he'd save thousands of dollars in fees, and he could take his time. His response was a week coming, but he finally agreed. I was thrilled beyond words, because one of Hollywood's top producers had agreed to read my book. On a Saturday afternoon, I sent the contract, Monday he signed it, and I started work that day.

The trade was a success for both of us. During the next thirty days, I contacted several dozen companies on behalf of the film company, and sure enough, Lucas read and provided feedback on what would eventually become Chambers. An epilogue is I took his advice, made dramatic changes and rewrites, and a year later, he optioned the entire series for a movie franchise.

Not all of my trades were so successful however. A friend owned a high-end web application development firm creating specialized business applications for F50 companies. He approached me about doing a trade for services: I'd complete partner development work on behalf of his company in return for creating a database of all the partnership information used by my company.

On the surface, it made sense. Developing a database would cost at least sixty-thousand dollars, money I'd never spend myself (I'm a big believer in spreadsheets), and it wasn't high on the priority list. We constructed the vision, and we both handed it off the internal managers for execution. The short and gruesome story is that we received a database so sophisticated that we gained very little value and suffered from lots of frustration, eventually mothballing it entirely. He, on the other hand, benefitted from the revenue-generating partnerships we had created for his firm. The lesson for us was to better scope out what we needed in the short term, as opposed to looking out so far in the future.

Ten Consulting Vocations

Are you comfortable in front of a crowd? Get paid to show others how to get top dollar by being a:

1. **Speaker Consultant**: consult individuals or groups how to stand, walk, gesture, use overheads and devices.
2. **Speaker Materials Consultant**: consult individuals or groups how to create the highest impact presentations for the right audience and forums.
3. **Media Consultant**: consult individuals or groups on how to interact with the media through interview role-playing, prepping, standing and answer deflection.
4. **New Executive Consultant**: consult individuals or groups on how to present themselves in corporate (and/or foreign) situations. This same consultant role can be tailored to government or non-profit environments.

5. **Speaker Bureau Consultant**: consult your client on how to become the next Tony Robbins by aligning your client with the right forum, pitching, and confirming speaking events.
6. **Author Presentation Consultant**: consult to authors (four million would-be authors exist in the United States alone) on how to perfect their speaking events in bookstores or to large audiences either consumer or corporate.
7. **Diversity Training Consultant**: consult with business clients on creating, implementing, and measuring diversity programs.
8. **Employee Claims Consultant**: consult to small businesses on behalf of your client––insurance firms—on how to lower liability claims through seminars and other training programs.
9. **Workplace Safety Consultant**: consult on new safety programs, policies, procedures, and establish a forum for measuring workplace safety.
10. **Corporate Etiquette and Skills Consultant**: consult to foreign companies seeking to conduct business in the United States on the culture and business etiquette for a demographic region or profession.

Action Items: Stage Four

✓ Consider the use of retainers, commissions and other fees in an engagement.

- ✓ If this appeals to most of your potential clients, work with the first couple to structure a balance between up front retainer money and back-end, revenue-associate payments.
- ✓ Use the first several clients to get it right before using this with prospects and clients.
- ✓ Utilize project or hourly rates when clients are most concerned with short term cash-flow and require the utmost flexibility.
- ✓ Trade for services judiciously, when you can afford it and when it makes sense for you and your client.
- ✓ Track, record and claim trade (or barter services to the IRS).
- ✓ Determine where your consulting firm should be located and what type of name will best serve your market and speak to your services.

Did you ever think you'd make it this far? Is your brain exploding with the possibilities of the future, or are you depressed that you've been missing other ways of generating income? Today is the day you start with fresh ideas and context for how others are making their own small businesses work for them. If you need to stop and pause to reflect on your business model, do so. It's the little adjustments you make in your business that can lead to great success, or faster demise.

We increased client revenue by $2.1 million in one year.

The Fifteen Group, a restaurant consultancy

Chapter Five: Telling Your Story

Founder and CEO David Hopkins of The Fifteen Group, launched his firm in 2001 after working with over thirty restaurants, ranging from nightclubs to fine dining. He has personally opened fifteen restaurants with budgets from $300,000 to more than 3 million, and his clientele list includes restaurateur Wolfgang Puck, who is prominently noted on his landing page.

All this from a man who was the classic overlooked expert, working at restaurants to achieve higher margins until he decided to make the leap to becoming a consultant to other businesses.

Millions of individuals work in restaurant marketing, a category that is divided into a variety of segments, from operational focus to concept and design, menu engineering and development, systems and procedures to accounting. Wait staff consulting training is such a large niche that it alone has hundreds of consulting firms. A search on the

Internet will return pages of restaurant and hospitality consultants (just ask Erika Spry).

What's different about David's approach is that he uses the combination of a dynamic website, customer quotes, success stories, and even seminars to generate leads and clients. David has a well-tuned machine that identifies, filters and delivers qualified prospects on a regular basis. Contrast his with Erika Spry, who doesn't want to travel and receives her clients from word-of-mouth, has no need or desire to have a fancy landing page.

The key to success for consultants in any business is to match the marketing approach and effort with the size and goals of the organization. Generating too much demand early on can break a business as easily as too little demand in later stages.

Data collection and staged marketing

David tracked return-on-investment metrics, such as client savings, which range between seven and fifteen percent of sales, or $70,000 and $150,000 on a restaurant with $1 million in sales. As his database of information grew, he refined his service offerings to match client requirements. For example, he showed how much menu engineering impacted margins. On annual food sales of $1M, David proved an increase of three percent on average, resulting in an additional $30,000.

That's a powerful metric, and with all the data he gathered, David grew his business in a thoughtful manner. At first, it was through direct marketing, then he offered free seminars to get in front of specific groups of potential customers.

Unfortunately, most consultants don't look at managed growth through staged marketing. Take the example of a Virginia-based consultant with expertise in gaining funding for non-profits (who wishes to remain anonymous). After years of writing funding grants and getting individual and corporate donations, he opened his own firm, and figured that the best way to generate new business was to send out a blanket direct mail.

He'd been advised by a marketing consultant to use a direct mail campaign to a database of affluent individuals in the surrounding zip code. He spent money for a three thousand-person list, and was pleased to announce that the first of a three-wave direct mail campaign was going to go out the following week.

Concerned, I asked him how many clients he could handle at any given time. His told me "Ten, maximum," and even that might be hard, due to the first and second meetings required before a client signed a check. The cycle was much longer for a complex grant.

It was my duty to tell him that he had better hope his return would fail to meet expectations or he would be overwhelmed. A great return would be about three percent, or ninety clients. An average return is one and a half percent, while a poor return is a half a percent. If his campaign were a complete failure at a half a percent, that still would mean he'd have fifteen clients, and he wouldn't be able to meet prospect demand.

Unfortunately, he was working with a marketing consultant who hadn't asked the critical questions regarding her client's ability to handle the results. He listened to her (and paid her the consulting fee required) and went ahead with the program.

The good news was the marketing consultant had created a great direct mail piece that effectively communicated his services. The bad news was that he was overwhelmed, as I had feared. He couldn't return all the inquiries in a timely manner (nearly forty, so congratulations to the consultant) but the sales cycles took longer than expected. In the end, he took on only six accounts, as other prospects looked for help elsewhere.

Staging a marketing campaign is crucial to early-state businesses. The key is to create enough awareness so you have lots of clients, and perhaps even a modest waiting list while not building market frenzy that can't be satisfied. The worst outcome is getting prospects hyped up about working with you and you not being able to return phones calls or schedule interviews. That will do nothing more than encourage those prospects to look to other sources providing the same services.

Local Marketing

New consultants can try a couple of different methods to generate awareness. The easiest and least expensive are local marketing efforts. This might start out with going to a local business event and announcing yourself.

When a male friend I've known since junior high school extended his insurance company from Oregon to Nevada, he attended the local Rotary at the invitation of his new banker. He gave a three-minute introduction, and when I Googled him a week after the event, I found the local business paper had written up a short blurb and included his photo. **He told me he set up a series of introductory meetings following**

the event, and the business was just enough to provide a base of clients. This was the start of word-of-mouth referrals.

Also, consider forums that represent your peers as well as your potential clients. As a consultant with a new business, every person you meet is a potential referral source.

- Business forums: city forums (Chamber of Commerce and Rotary)
- Business forums: private or organizational in nature
- Entrepreneur Organization (www.eo.org)
- Women's Entrepreneur Organization
- Forum for Women Entrepreneurs (www.fwe.org)
- Regional Entrepreneur's Forum, such as Northwest Entrepreneur Network (www.nwen.org)
- Universities and technical colleges

Marketing yourself to these forums is easy. You locate the speaker coordinator and send forth a speaker abstract.

A speaker abstract provides a summary about your services, why the audience needs someone of your abilities, a brief, three sentence pitch covering what you'd talk about, and then a fifty-word biography. This should include a current photo of you if available.

Keep in mind that a speaker abstract is appropriate for larger, more professional formats, and not usually the best for city or government sponsored events, where the interaction is more collegial. Farmers coming in from the fields to the weekly Rotary gathering aren't likely to be impressed by a dry slide presentation. Alternatively, three hundred professionals gathered together at an early-morning meeting will expect to be educated and enlightened, and to a degree, entertained.

Keep in mind, also, that event managers and specialists talk to one another and compare notes. Always give your best performance and add value with tips, techniques and other how-to's that expose your knowledge while adding value.

I can't emphasize this enough, since it's the reason why I graduated from non-paid events to getting paid and having a travel and expense budget.

It all started with pitching the Northwest Entrepreneur's Forum (NWEF) as a keynote speaker. No fee was offered, but the group of three hundred was full of potential clients, so I was happy to have the opportunity. Just after I left the stage, a woman on the board of the local Forum for Women Entrepreneurs (FEW) approached me to speak at an upcoming event. The group of thirty was far fewer than the NWEF (and didn't offer a fee), but I accepted nonetheless.

Among the group of women sat one man, who casually mentioned that he'd been invited to attend, and had done so because he needed to learn more about growing revenue through partnerships. At the end of the presentation, he provided me his card and asked whether I was interested in a consulting engagement with Microsoft. He worked in a different group from Tim Krause, one that none of my clients were interested in at the time. What's more: he wanted to hire me to help create a partnership plan, not find partners. That meant that for the first time, Microsoft the entity, would become a client.

This was a tremendous step forward for my small consulting firm, and it never would have come about had I not given my time free of charge at several events.

Laura King used events as a marketing tool in a slightly different way. As an organizational consultant, she first joined NAPO, the National Association Professionals Organization. By doing so, she was suddenly eligible to show up, introduce herself and start receiving client referrals. They meet up and share client projects at local chapter meetings.

One consultant will specialize on children's rooms while another will focus on kitchens. If they are doing an entire home, then they'll ask for someone in the vicinity with the specialty that's needed, and one or two will offer assistance. "It's a great way to share client opportunities," she said, glowing.

If you are an established speaker, you should go directly to Speakermatch and sign-up today.

Aligning Events with Your Consulting Specialty

Events can work for many industries, but not all. Animal therapist consultant Polly Klein, CEO Tonglen Healing Arts for Animals (www.tonglenhealingarts.com) based in Issaquah, Washington, found this out the hard way. Polly's earliest therapeutic practice was counseling families, where she focused her work on children living with cancer. Bringing this knowledge and training from her human counseling practice into her current healing work, Polly assists animals and people with understanding and resolving the emotional and energetic components of their behavioral and health issues.

After completing her degrees, teaching at Bastyr University for Craniosacral Therapy, and establishing her reputation as a nationally recognized animal communicator and healer, she thought events were a natural extension to build awareness for her consulting practice. Up to that point, Polly's business had grown through word-of-mouth referrals from veterinarians and educators, and directly from media coverage.

Polly invested her money in professional signage and made herself available for hours on end at these types of events, talking with people and sometimes offering a brief, free consultation. She even set up a raffle box to win a free, full consultations with her. But in the end, she almost never got a new client because of events, concluding it was a waste of her time.

"Clients come to me because I'm a known quantity, through referrals," she said. **"They weren't going to choose someone from a booth, without a personal reference, no matter how congenial I was or how great the signage was."**

Polly turned her attention to writing for prestigious publications in her field of expertise. She was readily accepted as a contributing editor thanks to her teaching position at Bastyr University. Between individuals who read her works and word-of-mouth referrals, it produced more than enough new business. Even so, she produces an electronic newsletter that can find its way into the hands of many potential clients and keep her name top of mind for prospects.

The Untapped Resources

Another free forum is the underutilized public library. **Using the public library system is the perfect forum to offer a free educational**

forum, open to the public, as a means of getting the word out. And let's face it: Joining a formal organization like NWEN and paying dues isn't for everyone. The public library system is a perfect forum to host your own program without any associated costs to you or the attendees.

The ground rules for using the public library are simple: No solicitation. So, don't go in expecting to sell anything or make a pitch. **Go in offering ideas to your target audience.** If you are an editorial consultant, you can offer a free hour-long workshop on how to self-edit the next great American novel. If you are a life coach, talk for an hour about the way to a more fulfilling home and family life. The list is endless.

Depending on the city in which you live, local publications will include a free announcement in the calendar section. All you do is schedule the event and place the information in the publications, and in return, you have generated awareness, used a free forum, and communicated your services to a new audience.

The next step up is perhaps partnering with a complimentary service provider to generate new business.

Consider the example of an attorney based in Seattle, WA, who specializes in employee law. She was approached by the owner of a mid-sized insurance company who realized his client premiums and corresponding number of claims might go down if the clients were better informed of the do's and don'ts of employee law. He suggested to the attorney they collaborate on a series of seminars where they'd both provide information to their mutual client base. This would extend each into the other's world in an unobtrusive, educational format. **It worked tremendously, yielding new clients for both entities.**

More importantly to the insurance CEO, his clients' claims went down, their company value increased and his clients were incredibly grateful for an insurance provider who went above and beyond "the norms" in the insurance industry to look after their business.

In another example, the life coach previously mentioned, partnered with a human resources consultant to hold free seminars at the local library. The local city paper posted the event notice on line and in the paper, and posters were also placed within the library itself and the community center. The only cost for the event itself was the food and beverages supplied on site.

The event was designed to help individuals improve their chances of employment by teaching a series of tips and techniques. About twenty-five individuals attended the first seminar, and each consultant gained one new client. **The following seminar, the attendee numbers nearly doubled, and both consultants gained a handful of clients**. It was enough to jumpstart a new set of client activity, and the next free seminar wasn't necessary until the following year.

Libraries have proven to be a great resource to identify new clients, so after the release of my first book, I scheduled a few local library events. Because the other events had been so well-attended, I didn't put much thought in to the promotion, giving myself a pass on the diligent placement in the calendar section of the local newspapers. This was the wrong time to be lazy. About five people showed, and I'd booked a large room, anticipating a full crowd. A well-attended event takes diligence and follow-through.

Advertising

Used wisely, advertising can be a superb vehicle for creating awareness, though it's not always guaranteed to generate demand. Confused? It's because in reality, advertising is more about making a company name or product familiar, so when you are standing at the counter, ready to decide, you feel confident in purchasing the product. That's advertising nirvana. The downside is that the volume of the advertising (*frequency*) must be loud and consistent to reach the consciousness of the intended recipient.

You can accomplish this by taking out four-color, full-page ads that will cost you a year's worth of work. **On the other hand, you could take out small, two-by-two-inch ads repeated every single week in one or two publications**.

In the early days of my consulting practice, about the time I was making enough to cover the bills and put a bit into a marketing fund, I made the decision to advertise in *The Red Herring.* While relatively small in circulation, it was a must-read by the venture capitalists and the start-up firms they funded; my target clients.

It was rather expensive, yet I committed to a six-month run. My two-color, full-page ad had a single, large image of a maze in shades of gray, with a red line weaving its way through and out the other side. The tagline read: Helping you through the partnership maze. The three sentences below talked about wanting to partner with an organization without getting burned, along with a description of our services. It was simple, blunt, and included the business phone number.

The point wasn't to field ten thousand phone calls. It was to establish a presence that would make it a bit easier when I cold-called a company, requesting an audience with the chief executive or senior vice president of business development.

A funny thing happened because of the ad. One day, I received a call from David Kirkpatrick, then a senior technology writer at *Fortune Magazine*, calling me because he'd seen my ad. He thought it was amazing that a consultant would provide services for outsourced partner development, and even more amazed that I was making a living at it! At the time, I was still in my paranoid stage and practically begged him to ignore the ad and go away. He told me, in the kindest of ways, that he thought there was a story lurking behind the ad, and I could help him or not, but he was going to write about it anyway.

This is where advertising and public relations merged. **The advertising was a tactical approach to creating name awareness for my company. The public relations part happened by accident when an editor saw it as a story idea.**

This was a gift from God, as I had neither budget nor intent to engage in a public relations effort and certainly not one that included top-flight business publications. Yet, it was an opportunity I couldn't refuse, and it lifted my business off the ground within days of the article's appearance. That year, my second full year in business, revenues tripled from approximately $120,000 to nearly $600,000 and continued to double for the following two years. To this day, nearly a dozen years later, I still have executives contacting me, referencing the article in *Fortune*.

Once I'd decided to advertise in the Red Herring, I hired a graphic designer to create the imagery. When the bill came, I paid the designer $2,500 for the work, believing I owned the imagery, as it was created for me. After the ad appeared, the designer called and scolded me for using "her images without paying." Wasn't that what I paid for?" I asked. No, she responded. I had paid for one-time use. To remedy this, I had to pay another $1,500 for unlimited usage. I also learned to double check usage terms.

Public Relations

Traditional public relations starts with writing a press release that gives the media a story idea, along with enough details so an editor or reporter can make a decision to cover the piece. Once a release is written, it must be distributed to the various media outlets. **This is where a consultant must use caution and monitor the pocketbook at the same time**. Sending a press release to the local newspaper is free and can be done by email, often to the editor in charge of that section, such as the business editor or entertainment editor. Nearly all media outlets now provide specific directions on how and when to submit a press release, along with the caveat they don't guarantee a response.

When the release has a broader regional slant, outlets from two or three states might make a story of the release. In situations where the story has a national scope, the Associated Press (AP) might write an article, and then media outlets around the country that subscribe to the AP choose whether to run the story as is.

Knowing that **the average editor of even a small publication receives fifty to a several hundred press releases a week, it's important to cultivate a relationship with that person ahead of the release**

distribution. It's this contact who ensures the press release is at least looked at and considered for a story, as opposed to being immediately dismissed and thrown into the round file under the desk. However, if the story idea itself isn't worthy of coverage, an article isn't going to appear, regardless of the relationship.

The media pinwheel includes local print, radio and television, as well as cable. If you are in a mid-sized metropolitan area, it might be regional, incorporating several cities or states. The ability to reach an editor directly is inversely proportional to the size of the city or town in which you live. The larger the city, the harder it is to get access to the editor. The smaller the city, the easier it is.

Five cities with seven different publications exist within a fifteen-mile radius of where I reside. Each has three editors, focusing on news, the calendar, and the community. After contacting all the editors and providing them story ideas for the past six months, I finally approached the editor in my home town about my last book.

Fortunately for me, it was a slow news period, and I landed on the front cover of the publication. This was on the stands for three days until it the next issue appeared. **It was about seven months from the time I first contacted this editor to establish a relationship, but only three days from the time I pitched my own story and received press coverage**. Start delivering value to the editor of the local paper on topics other than yourself. When the time comes for you to be covered yourself, you will have the relationship established.

I learned something else when dealing with the local papers, and that's they generally only cover events that occur within specific zip codes and profile individuals living within those same boundaries. After just a few weeks of feeding other outlets ideas, I figured out that only one would be interested in my story, yet I maintained the relationships with the other editors. I knew that at some point, I'd give seminars in those areas, or can use the contacts, and now I have.

The personal relationship with a member of the media is sometimes the most vital to success

---

After the *Fortune* piece appeared, I announced the licensing, distribution, and investment deals I'd created for clients, making them the center point of the press release. Each one included quotes from the client(s), the work and the expected results. Only a single line in the beginning and end mentioned the role of my firm in the partnership deal. It was enough. The follow-on public relations continued the media coverage to include publications like *Inc. Magazine*, *Entrepreneur Magazine* and others.

Generating Story Ideas

The story of YOU is fresh only once. After that, you must get creative. You can twist and turn your consulting practice into stories that center on everything from events to holidays or your clients. Here are a few ideas:

- **Client success stories.** Nothing sells your success like a company (your client) who can tell the world how they were struggling before you arrived, how you helped them, and how much more successful they are because of your work.

- **Event-driven slant**. If you are a bridal consultant, concoct a story about trends for brides in time for the local bridal fair, and send the editors pictures of your clients.
- **Staged events**: In the Northwest, a lot of boating consultants are hired to find, develop, and manage personal watercraft, such as yachts. One consultant told me of an annual promotional tour he created just for editors to showcase a client's boat, akin to the before-and after presented in *Architectural Digest Magazine*. After several years, this featured section became the who's who of boating in the Northwest, and this consultant was the most valuable resource.
- **Charity- or benefit-driven activities**. Select an organization that provides a worthy service to the community, or one that's aligned with your personal beliefs and is identifiable to the media and do something for free. For the first book in my time-travel adventure series, I held a book reading at the Children's Hospital. The point wasn't press or sales of a book. It was something I did because I feel strongly about the services offered by Children's. It turned out that the parents of one of the children told the media, and the hospital took some photos. The photos ended up in the press, but it was completely unintentional.
- **Co-promote an event**. Moving to a home office caused me to evaluate the local businesses in the area with whom to partner for an event. A local small-business copy center was happy to supply the space and promote two free seminars on small business marketing techniques. The exposure was incredible, and the copy

center differentiated itself as a provider of value-added services. Here again, the local media turned up to cover the event, since it involved two businesses, and a free education for the community.

Consider the possibilities of applying any of these public relations strategies to your own business. Can you partner with other local businesses? Are you complimentary to consultants or businesses with the same target market and demographic? How can you incorporate local media into your efforts?

Industry-Specific Public Relations

If your clients are across the country and you can handle an influx of prospects, then your public relations efforts may can be national. If that's the case, your target industry might also have specific magazines that you can approach for press coverage.

Think about trade show management. As a part of my marketing background, I spent several years managing trade show activities for an employer on a global basis. I knew the ins and outs of event management, and my education was due in part to the half-dozen publications tailored to this market.

Had I elected to start a business consulting to other firms about trade shows, I would have sought out the editors of these publications and offered to write a by-line column for free, just to get the name recognition. Additionally, I would have provided my biographical information and offered myself up as an expert source in an area for their reporters to call upon for quotes. Again, the expert source designation can be worth thousands of dollars in free publicity. Once the media starts quoting you on a regular basis, you can add this to your biography. You'd be surprised how comforting it is for a client to know that others have validated your expertise. This also means you can charge a bit more for your services.

It's easy enough to find publications for each target market. Personally, I saved myself the $3,000 fee charged by media tracking companies and went directly to Yahoo!'s directory of publications. It lists on- and off-line media outlet by category, from non-profit publications through manufacturing.

If you aren't prepared to write (by-line) an article, the very best stories for vertical industry publications are client success stories, so share those during the introductory phone call or shortly thereafter.

Knowledge-Based Articles

For a consultant with deep expertise in a technical field, such as science or medicine, writing an article that's educational and informative. It can lead to a dramatically accelerated business.

Take the experience of Dr. Richard Satava. Dr. Satava is employed as a surgeon at the University of Washington, Seattle. He is also a consultant and advisor to the government of the United States on warfare and advance technology as well as numerous private organizations.

Dr. Satava has expertise in funding, and reviews hundreds of advanced biomedical technology research projects while maintaining an active surgical practice. He elaborates on the difference between himself and others in his field.

"While some doctors perform research while they practice medicine, few have the combination of clinical practice, active research, funding, and business experience."

Like Becky Bishop and Polly Klein, Dr. Satava's skills and perspective were overlooked for a short period, until he started writing articles for medical journals.

Dr. Satava began by publishing his own research projects, as well as those he funded. The result? **Companies interested in learning more about these advanced technologies and the impact on their business sought him out.** About the same time, Dr. Satava began receiving invitations to speak at conferences and symposiums. This begat a consulting business, because clients read his work, then later heard him lecture and wanted him to provide the same kind of information to their company.

When the federal government realized that Dr. Satava had a first look at new medical technology, he was asked to advise the Department of Defense. Now, Dr. Satava consults to the Department of Defense, within the Medical Research Command, and he is the senior advisor to the commanding general on advanced technologies for healthcare and the battlefield.

Then an interesting new area of opportunity emerged. As Dr. Satava learned the processes, procedures, and techniques of working with the government, he added yet another consulting business.

"Sometimes it is helping a small business submit a Small Business Innovation Research (SBIR) solicitation, to simply having a short meeting with their company." In other cases, consulting on governmental operations consists of moderating a workshop the client is conducting for a group of employees.

For the record, Dr. Satava maintains his primary job as a surgeon, his consulting job for the government, and then a consulting practice for non-governmental entities. And all of this has stemmed from leveraging his knowledge and research efforts to taking advantage of writing and placing articles and industry-specific papers.

Beyond Print

Radio stations don't have the same editorial requirements of print. **In fact, local radio coverage can be easier to achieve than print coverage.** The only downside to a consultant is that this coverage can throw the doors open so wide, it's the same problem as a successful direct mail campaign.

Leverage radio coverage by selecting stations that offer programs targeted to your audience. For example, in Los Angeles, several radio programs are for men only. The topics range from relationships to cars and just about everything in between. Consultants, psychologists, manicurists, and management experts have all been featured on the shows. If you're a life coach specializing in men's issues, these might be great shows for you.

The biggest benefit of radio is its real time and affordable. **Many interviews are conducted over the phone, so you can be at home, providing your commentary.** In one case, after my book on partnerships was published, I sought out radio programs geared toward small businesses. The University of Shenandoah sponsors one such radio program, and the host is a professor in the school of entrepreneurship. He called for our on-air interview, and I happened to be camping. Talk about convenient public relations.

When this radio show aired, I wasn't worried about being inundated with new prospects, since the bandwidth of the listenership was narrow, covering only about sixty thousand listeners in Virginia. And sure enough, the twelve-minute interview didn't generate a single inbound phone call or email. Yet, it was a great piece which I posted on the website, and it garnered several more publicity opportunities than it did yield new clients.

Web Marketing

When you created your firm and constructed a website, you set the foundation for Internet marketing. Unless you want to travel outside your region, then your initial efforts should be focused on linking sites with complimentary service providers in the local area. Think about a bridal design consultant. This person could have web links with florists, hair salons, retail outlets, and apparel retail stores. **A referral fee, also known as an affiliate program, could be offered and put in place for any money that changes hands.**

Another type of web marketing is posting your company on site like Craigslist.com (www.craigslist.com). This site is a perfect service for listing a job opening, but also for posting your own services.

While writing this book, I needed a book jacket designer. Six months ago, I would have Googled designers and my city and seen what popped up. This time, I went straight to Craigslist under services, and trolled several categories, including creative and computers, since

I've found that designers fluent in web design tend to list in both places.

In less than five minutes, I found a few designers who had placed announcements of their services. I queried both with the details of my project, and the response was within minutes for one, and a couple of hours for the other. After reviewing both proposals, I selected one, and we quickly came to an agreement on an hourly rate of twenty-five dollars with a not-to-exceed amount that fit my budget, and she started work the following morning.

Mike Konesky has had a lot of success in setting up saved job searches on monster.com which yield new prospective clients.

"I can get a pretty good, daily automatic e-mail sent to me that shows which companies are looking to hire for specific roles that my firm might be able to take on," he explained. Then he follows up with the companies either directly or through monster.com, to initiate a conversation about the potential benefits of working with his firm.

The flip side of working with job boards is if you're not careful, you can get pulled into situations that can take up a lot of time but aren't good clients. This happens if you post a résumé or CV on a site and allow all users to view and access your posting, something that Konesky recommends against.

List serves are another vehicle for new client generation. During the course of writing my various books, I've asked my friends in the publishing business to post a 'for hire' note on the appropriate list serve. This has run the gamut from editorial consulting to technical editing, proofreading and line editing.

Since I'm not a consulting editor of any kind, I don't have access to these list serves. Working through a third party who's a known entity on the list serve, I get access to an incredible network of skilled consultants. They, on the other hand, have a viable prospective client—me!

The last element of a list serve is that members are uncommonly active, and seemingly on the scout for new projects at all times of the day or night. Case in point: when my friend who belonged to a list serve did me a favor and posted a note for a copy editor, I had over forty interested editorial consultants respond directly to me within two hours. From this, I selected three editors for different projects, and each one was between $400 and $800. Being on a list serve paid big dividends for those that I chose simply by being listed.

Check out list serves that address your consulting expertise, get on them and stay active. They might produce a nice bit of business with very little effort.

Ten Consulting Vocations

Did you wait tables through college or are you doing so now? Like many overlooked experts, you may have a lot to offer a growing business. It's all about packaging your services in a way that's easily understood by your target client. Have you worked in politics or the military? You have quite a few options.

1. **Wait staff Consultant**: consult restaurant owners on how to hire and train staff to dramatically improve revenue.
2. **Menu Engineering Consultant**: consult with chefs on the best food menus to produce the highest per plate spend, better margins and improved customer services.
3. **Restaurant Design Consultant**: consult developers of food establishments on proven floor plans for specific types of restaurants, designs and themes for maximum service and revenue.
4. **Kitchen Design Consultant**: consult with restaurant owners directly, or collaborate with a master contractor as a part of the restaurant design team.
5. **Institutional Food Consultant**: consult to organizations such as large corporations with in-house service, nursing homes, hotels, hospitals and other facilities on all aspects (or just a few) food areas.
6. **Staged Marketing Consultant**: consult with clients on the best marketing and sales strategies to grow their business for specific stages of business.
7. **Government Procurement Consultant**: consult to clients desiring to sell products or services to the government.
8. **Military Device Consultant**: consult to government or corporate clients on the best devices to utilize on the field or in a corporate defense setting.
9. **Medical Technology Consultant**: consult to government on the best technology to utilize in the field, or conversely, consult to

corporate (non-government entities) on what products they could and should sell to the government.

10. **Political Consultant**: consult to existing or potential candidates on strategy, messages and positioning for small county races, regional, state or national elections. This could also include consulting clients on how to better work with city commissioners, parks and recreation, or other governmental agencies.

Action Items: Stage Five

- ✓ Start your marketing efforts using free venues, such as libraries. Offer educational forums to establish credibility and build a referral network.
- ✓ Use advertising to create name-brand awareness in a very narrow market. Expect to continue a campaign for at least six months.
- ✓ Partner with other complimentary service providers to grow your referral base gradually.
- ✓ Consider public relations to extend coverage in a staged manner, starting first with local, then regional, and then national coverage.
- ✓ Don't overlook the potential to write a by-line or contributor article to establish you as an industry or subject matter expert.

- ✓ Web and Internet marketing is foundational. Selectively choose other Internet sites and establish bi-directional links to their sites.

Overwhelmed with the types, scope and details of available marketing programs? Of the options I've listed, **filter it down to what you want to do and what you may be good at,** be it speaking in front of others, writing an article or partnering for a free event at the local library. You can do at least one of those things, and do it well. You have time to build up your "marketing" skills, those that may not come naturally, but are essential to the long-term success of your business.

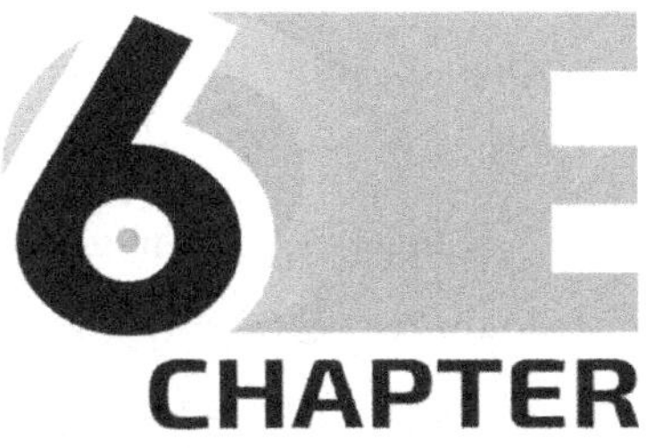

The best practice is to follow the advice posted on every railroad crossing. Stop. Look. Listen.

Sam Keen

Chapter Six: Methods and Best Practices

A methodology is a set of underlying principles or practices for any given industry, a task or multi-step effort. When the term *best practices* is placed in front of *methodology*, it refers to a process or set of processes that has been proven, time and again, to provide a predictable, or known, set of outcomes. Usually, best practices also imply a shorter time to accomplish the task, lower cost, lower risk, and a higher level of satisfaction.

You will find that firms small and large apply best practices although they may rarely use the phrase. Likely as not, a painter would simply say: "We're experts, and we'll save you money and do the job faster; look at the ten houses we've painted, and talk to the owners." A technology consultant might tell the client to: "Use proven, best-practices methodologies to yield predictable outcomes. Here, read our client success stories." A retired pastor who consults to churches about setting up, structuring, building and operating a new church has a very specific process to follow as well, but uses different words.

On average, an independent consultant in process methodology field makes nearly fifty-thousand dollars a year. To be hired, he/she must be able to talk through the steps to prospective clients, just as a landscape architect, office organizer or puppy trainer.

I can't always change the direction of the wind, but I can adjust my sails to always reach my destination.

Jimmy Dean

Create Once, Reuse, Refine

The best way to create a methodology is to track and record every little step in the process. This includes (but isn't limited to) what you say, when you say it, what you write, what you present, how and when you present it, the emails you send and receive along with the dependencies upon others, the meetings that are required—and the list goes on and on. It's encouraging, then, that this only must be done once. After that, the process is refined over and over.

Beyond saving time for future clients, a methodology can be summarized or simplified. You look incredibly organized in front of your clients as you provide a guide to what they can expect throughout your engagement. For an organizational consultant, her methodology is five steps and simply articulated:

1. An on-site visit to your office, home or area to be organized
2. Prepare a visual of the proposed space design
3. Sign the contract, purchase the materials as necessary and schedule a date(s) for installment/change
4. Review and approve with the client
5. Final sign-off and payment

One may consider this a business process, but in fact, it's her *best practice* for ensuring project success. By the way, this exact process is found in many service businesses. Unsurprisingly, the length and detail of the method used is in direct correlation to the complexity of the project. Mike Konesky has a multi-page methodology for different types of applications he develops.

Beyond the client project at hand, a process methodology can be repurposed to train other consultants you hire to work on a project or even contractors. Rather than relying upon your knowledge (thereby making you the bottleneck), the items used throughout a project (e.g., written documents or spreadsheets) are as good as, and sometimes better for the other individuals working on the assignments.

Types and Formats

If you are new to using a methodology, it's helpful to understand what format your clients would prefer before you spend the money in a system that won't be adopted.

As an example, because I spent a lot of time working with Microsoft, they had a specific request that I use Microsoft Project Plan. I had to purchase the software and convert all my process flows to this desktop application. Yet, when I went to use the same methodologies with other clients, I found that maybe fifty percent used Microsoft Project Plan.

My solution was to create a master document in Project Plan, so if a client used this application, I customized the document as necessary. If the client didn't use Project Plan, I'd convert the document to a PDF and send it via e-mail as well as print it out and bring it to meetings.

In other cases, where the client wanted the electronic file to track the project, but neither had, nor wanted to purchase and learn Microsoft Project, I'd use the export the document to a Microsoft Excel spreadsheet. This was particularly helpful in situations where multiple contributors across different teams were participating in the project. Then the point person for the client could update and change status of individual items.

I'll give you an example. FileNet Corp is a billion-dollar software firm based in Los Angeles. I was hired to manage a product withdrawal from the market. At the time, I'd launched products but had never removed one. I was upfront with the client about the fact I'd not actually done this before, but we both felt confident I could work with the legal team, the product teams, and customer service to complete the program.

This was the perfect opportunity for me to create a methodology. Using a Microsoft Excel spreadsheet, I worked with the program manager at the client site, each meeting brought forth new tasks that required dependencies with multiple business units. Over a six-month period, nearly twenty-five business groups were involved, from finance, legal, marketing, sales, product development, distribution and channel, inventory, and manufacturing. Every e-mail that was distributed, voice mail sent, legal document created, and even executive presentation made, was identified, prioritized and tagged for the timeline, and then assigned to an owner who created the deliverable. The final methodology included 300+ line items of tasks.

The process methodology was used as a guide throughout the actual withdrawal. When the program was officially completed at the end of twelve months, the document itself became the master for my consulting firm. FileNet also retained its version for future use.

Using the Data Points Gathered by a Methodology

One of the facets of tracking the outcomes of a project is parlaying this into data points that can be used in marketing and sales efforts. This is done when you have established a baseline for a project, then over time, you can show that by using your method, the outcomes are dramatically better.

In the case of my initial work with Microsoft, Tim Krause was more than willing to share with me the data points surrounding the partnering efforts of his group. This gave me a baseline for the goals I wanted to beat with my services. As the project commenced and milestones were met, I noted the time and cost, then upon project completion, verified all the data with my client counterpart. These included:

- Time to create a partnership with Microsoft: 6 to 9 months
- Number of meetings before a yes/no decision was made by Microsoft: 5
- Average cost to the partner from the first call to the time an agreement was signed: Minimum of $15,000 on average

- Average return on investment from the partnership: Less than $50,000
- Average number of individuals contacted at Microsoft before the right person was found: 12
- Average number of phone calls the partner had to make before finding the right contact: over 30

If you are shaking your head, you aren't alone. Those are some pretty dismal data points. Yet it gave me a starting point for metrics that I'd want to beat using my own processes and improve partner satisfaction.

If I could prove that my consulting methodologies bettered these data points, then I would use this information as a selling point for other groups at the company.

It took six months and a handful of clients, but I demonstrated I could reduce this timeframe to partnership to three months (versus six). This dropped the cost per partnership effort to less than $5,000 (that means a savings of $10,000). The average return on investment tripled, to more than $150,000, and the number of meetings to reach a decision dropped from five to one. This last data point is significant. By collapsing multiple meetings into one, attended by many decision makers, the cost to my client was dramatically reduced, and the return on investment skyrocketed. Lastly, the total, average number of Microsoft contacts was upwards of thirty, not twelve.

While the clients were thrilled, those we worked with at Microsoft were equally pleased. They had pre-qualified partners being hand-guided through the internal process. The partners came to the meetings prepared, issues and potential conflicts easily resolved, smoothing the way for a partnership to get started far quicker than if they were working on their own.

> **Author Note**: At this point, I want to clearly state I'm not selling my business services as I've stepped away from day-to-day partnership development activities and am spending my time on sharing what I've learned through writing. Take this example, and the others I'm relating as real examples of what can and should be realized as you work and build your own business.

Methodologies aren't always necessary

Dr. Satava believes in process methodologies for his medical work, but not when it comes to either of his consulting practices. He believes each one would be hindered if he were constrained by a methodology.

"There is no defined process because the requests are usually very different," he explains. The application of his knowledge is attuned to a specific client need or decision. This doesn't lend itself to a defined input and output mechanism.

This is also true with the life coach, who says: "I take each individual client as its own project, not a one size fits all."

Using a methodology has an added advantage of enabling you to name a process (or service product) and attach a fixed price. On the other hand, if your consulting practice hinges on unique situations, like either of Dr. Satava's consulting practices, creating and using a methodology is impossible.

Ten Consulting Vocations

Were you a gear-head in high school shop or did you work the front desk for an automobile dealer? Perhaps you worked on the other side of the automotive industry, providing appraisals for an insurance company. Each of these skills has an associated level of knowledge about cars, business processes and value for an automobile.

1. **Appraisal Consultant**: consult to body shops, dealers and independent insurance companies on the value of a car, or car repair costs.
2. **Sourcing Consultant**: consult on automotive parts, rework, containment and inspection services.
3. **Customer Lifecycle Management Consultant**: consult on solutions for warranty, service parts, repair management, service contracts and fleet services.
4. **Car Wash Consultant**: consult about the best formats, features, and price points in this highly lucrative niche.
5. **Manufacturer Consultant**: consult to small businesses and start-up clients desiring to break into the automotive or transportation industry.
6. **Architectural Consultant**: consult small parts or other new automotive businesses and surrounding industries on store design.
7. **Civil Engineering Consultant**: consult with private companies about how to best work with county, city or state regulatory agencies.

8. **Acoustical Design Consultant**: consult home (or office) builders and designers on the latest technology used in automobiles, devices and home equipment.
9. **Customer Service Consultant**: consult small and midsize companies on all aspects of customer service, identifying the correlation between loss of client and loss of revenue, to the increased revenue and margin of client retention.
10. **Overseas Call Center Consultant**: consult to foreign organizations on how to acquire new clients in a specific demographic region or vertical industry.

Action Items: Stage 6

- ✓ Determine whether a methodology is required for your consulting service.
- ✓ Create a bullet point process that you can repeat (which you may already be doing as a part of the sales process).
- ✓ If extensive, develop a more sophisticated list, perhaps in a spreadsheet such as one offered by Google docs, which can be shared with your clients.
- ✓ Validate the format desired by the client, and if the methodology is proprietary and will be owned by the client.
- ✓ Determine if this can be used as a competitive differentiator and allow you to charge a premium.
- ✓ Utilize this process document for internal training or with contractors you may hire for your project.

If you pick the right people and give them the opportunity to spread their wings and put compensation as a carrier behind it, you almost don't have to manage the people.

Jack Welch

Chapter Seven: Getting the Most from Your Team

Visualize a time when your business has a steady stream of clients, your profit margins are excellent, and your quality of life is high. Then add to the scene three more prospects knocking at your door, each one representing the opportunity to have fun, maintain great margins, and offer a high probability of succeed. What do you do?

Option one: You put the clients on a wait list, keeping the commitment to your existing client(s) that your service won't diminish.

Option two: You take on the project(s) yourself, extending the timeframe of each, knowing it will be a physical and mental stretch, but believe it's a better choice than turning the opportunity down cold.

Option three: You hire a full-time headcount who will be perfect for the three engagements, knowing full well that you will have to train this newcomer, and then be burdened with the requirement of keeping this person busy after the immediate engagements end.

Option four: You hire a contractor on a project basis, with the vision that your project load will be relatively steady, and that the contractor will be around when you need the resource.

Chuck Pryor's success at his first business forced him to make a decision early in the process.

"In the beginning," said Chuck, "I could put out the equipment myself and have it ready to go, then run the show." But success brought with it the necessity to hire contractors. "I had a choice to make. I either hired on contractors for the event or I was going to forever be doing the small shows and never graduate."

To keep costs low and flexibility high, he hired contractors who worked on a per project basis. "Once I showed them what I expected and how I worked, I'd hire them time and again." For years, in fact, right up until he sold the business, he never had to hire a full-time employee.

"I wasn't doing it full-time myself, so wasn't going to sign up to have staff around to wait for the weekends, when most of the major musical events happen," he explained. This wasn't due to a lack of interest from clients, he points out. "Quite frankly, I had enough business to do gigs during the week, but I loved being on the radio then and I love it now, that's my first calling. I wasn't going to have that business intrude."

The downside of this choice was that sometimes he couldn't get enough people to hold an event on the weekend. In those rare cases, he reached out to his competitors.

"It's a pretty tightly-knit community of music professionals," Chuck continued, "so we'd help each other out." That meant sharing resources and sharing money.

"When a two-hour event is earning you thousands or tens, there's more than enough to share."

Hiring Options & Profit Margins

The goal of any business is to maintain strong profit margins, no matter the circumstances. After working for one of the largest consulting organizations in the world, co-owning his own consultancy, then working at a small boutique, Mike Konesky has seen all four approaches in action. Now, when he faces a client-overload, Mike also opts to contract with other specialists on a project basis.

"I'll bring in one or two consultants based on specific projects. This gives me the flexibility to hire the very best for a particular engagement, instead of having a consultant that's a one-size-fits-all." Being light and agile helps Mike stay focused on what is important for him and the goals of his company.

It also allows him to maintain the profit margins he has set for the specific client project.

"I saw through experience when I worked for other corporations that the margins quickly eroded when the first rule of lowering the project price happened. It's like a spiral effect, where the client manager would do anything to "get the project" and pretty soon we had the project but no room for a profit."

Mike handles the scenario by having a very straightforward conversation with the client, which goes something like this. "I'll say—look, we want the project, but the way it's scoped, you need N number of people and so on. If I under bid the project, it leaves no lee-way for me to meet my company goals." Mike says this type of honest conversation works wonders with the client.

"They know I'm running a business too, and if I'm working for such low margins, I might short-cut the work or rush through the program development, which is the last thing they want. Typically, a compromise is worked out, but I still am within my comfort zone for the price and margins."

Basic margins can be determined by such details as the cost of the consultant time, your billing rate, the cost of materials, and travel.

In one case, BMG was contracted by Network Appliance (www.netapp.com) to provide an on-site team leadership session around partner strategies. This required a senior director and myself. It wasn't that I couldn't do the job alone. Rather, I had three other goals in mind that I wanted to accomplish, and it was impossible for one just consultant.

First, I wanted the best customer experience possible. An all-day session can be mentally fatiguing for both the consultant and client, particularly when managing a dynamic, and sometimes aggressive, group of more than ten individuals who are together for multiple, consecutive sessions. Meeting participants grow bored of hearing the same voice and unconsciously turn off or tune out. This is the last thing a consultant wants in a meeting.

Second, I wanted my senior director (a contractor consultant), to establish a relationship with NetApp directly, so he could lead future projects. At the time, I was the only advisor from my company whom the client had worked with on strategic engagements. My contact had warned me that he was wary of me "passing him off to a junior associate." As NetApp was a four-hour plane ride away, I didn't mind an occasional trip, but didn't want to be beholden to fly down for every single meeting. I assured him the man was a senior executive.

Taking this approach would help me accomplish my last goal, which was to attain future contracts with this contractor as the project lead. If we could split efforts and maintain the margins I'd set, this would effectively double the company revenue.

At the end of this client session, my direct contact, a vice president, took me aside and asked me about two other potential assignments. Our conversation centered around my rates versus those of my associate, who had suitably impressed the client. I would charge a much lower rate for him (in the $1,500 range) than for myself (which ran between $5-7,500). Even after what I'd pay out, I'd be making a healthy margin, and could take on another client engagement.

The secret of my success is that we have gone to exceptional lengths to hire the best people in the world.

Steve Jobs

Backlogging Clients

Backlogging isn't much more than scheduling out the start of an engagement, much like booking a dentist appointment. This can be several weeks to a month or two out. The benefits of this approach include the ability to identify and confirm your staffing. **The downside is that the client can back out during the thirty days unless you have a signed contract and a small retainer.**

If you are going to employ the backlog strategy, you need to prepare against the reality your prospect might cancel after you have lined up your own staff. You do this by requesting a portion of the total fee upon contract signing. **A rule of thumb is ten to twenty percent of the total fee is paid upon signing of the contract**. This is applied toward the program when it starts, however, if the engagement is cancelled, and you aren't informed at least (ten days, two weeks- you decide) prior to the start of the engagement, you keep that money. Alternatively, you can choose to keep a percentage, say five percent, as non-refundable, and the other amount is prorated. It all comes down to what you will owe to your contractors or other expenses you might have incurred and need to cover.

Hiring Full-Time Consultants

Making the investment to hire a full-time resource within a small business is a significant commitment of resources, if you include recruiting, educating, and training efforts; and of money, considering salaries, benefits, and other incentives. Weighing the advantages against the challenges is the only way to know whether hiring is the best option for your situation.

It was six months after I started BMG that I faced the decision to hire a full-time headcount or a contractor. By then, I'd found backlogging was more challenging than I'd thought. I realized the opportunity cost of losing the engagement was higher than the cancellation fee paid to me. In other words, the opportunities I'd passed up were sometimes worth more than the backlogged client program I accepted. To make matters worse, those very same opportunities were gone when I called to reinvigorate the project.

Then I attempted to manage the clients on my own, which worked to a point. I learned I could handle around three to five clients, depending on the size and scope. If the projects were extensive, my client roster dropped to a single engagement, which significantly raised my risk, as it placed the burden of all costs covered by a single entity. Faced with a growing business, I made the choice to hire a full-time employee.

Backlogging projects is a nice notion, but too much can change in thirty days to justify setting aside the resources. Make sure your cancellation fee is high enough to cover the opportunity cost.

Efficiency

It takes the same amount of time to post, review, and hire either a consultant or full-time employee. I estimated that it would take at least one, and potentially several engagements to train a recruit properly on our methodologies. It would come down to the specialization in partner development and techniques used across industries or types of deals.

Since establishing a new market niche, I was overly wary of giving away trade secrets to a consultant who could potentially set up shop and compete with me, a young, shallow-pocketed consultant with no ability to sue for intellectual property theft.

Margins and Consultant Philosophy

Paying a salary to the contractor would be steep, unless I could hire a professional with a few years' experience who could be trained and honed into a top-notch consultant. With a backlog of only six months of projects, I couldn't afford to commit to a contract longer than that timeframe. Further, a seasoned consultant might be married to past methodologies and perhaps not be open to my own way of doing business. This fit my margin requirement as well as my long-term goals of the personalities within the consultancy.

Client Consistency

The best engagements have a single point of contact from beginning to end. When you hire someone who can qualify, then develop and manage the relationship, you are free to expand your own efforts for the company. Under your tutelage, your full-time employee is invested in the client for multiple projects, not just one. In fact, it's reasonable to expect that one of the goals of the full-time employee is to identify and close additional projects from the client.

Avoiding the Bait and Switch

When a prospective client is being pitched, it's not uncommon to have one person (the most articulate and knowledgeable) to be different from the individual(s) doing the work. Small businesses rarely have this luxury (the owner is usually the main contact), yet the concern that a bait and switch will take place is common.

"The best way to address this is right up front," said Mike Konesky. He addresses this during his two-day, no-charge project assessment. If another consultant is required, Konesky conveys communicates this to the client during the assessment phase, and the introduction is made before or at the project kickoff meeting.

Keeping Great Talent

Before I started my own firm, I was as guilty as the next person of poaching the advertising, public relations, and other sales and marketing firms' excellent employees. The rift was temporary, since whatever corporation I was working for had a steady stream of agency work. **When I decided to hire full-time employees, talent poaching was high on my list of worries, and I set out to ensure that I'd keep the employees I'd hire**. This included a combination of monetary incentives, as well as professional-development perks that were not normally available to young professionals.

When your employees are happy, they are your very best ambassadors.

James Sinegal, co-founder, Costco

Uncommon Incentives

Owners of small businesses need to be creative when it comes to enticing employees to stick around after a project is completed. **Depending on your philosophy and the compensation structure you have with your clients, you might be surprised at what you can divvy up for employee incentives**.

At nineteen, I was already working in the software industry. I envied the employees who received stock options (I was told that anyone under 21 couldn't receive stock or participate in 401K), and I really turned green when the sales people received bonuses and trips to Mexico as a part of the rewards program.

Why was it, I wondered, that only the sales representatives got to go on the trips? And why didn't the receptionists get to share in the commissions when a big deal closed? After all, wasn't it the receptionist who'd taken the phone calls, booked the plane, and dealt with angry customers? Because I'd witnessed these perceived injustices for several years, I made the decision to share the wealth long before I started my business. Here's what I did, and how it worked out.

Company Ownership and Sharing the Big Wins

As an S corporation, my firm was limited in the ability to give employees shares and dividends. It could have been done, but I'd need the attorneys every time I hired a new employee and changed the corporate papers. At a few hundred bucks an hour, my attorney wisely suggested that I use another means to accomplish my goal, which was profit sharing.

The first tools to use were the stock options that the company received from clients as a part of the program fee. As I'd been an employee of software companies that had either been purchased or gone public, I had already benefited from options grants. With my own firm, I often negotiated stock options as a part of the compensation mix. My goal was to give a part of the stock away to my full-time employees, and that's what I accomplished. Here are the details of how I structured it with the clients first, and then how I provided it to my employees.

The Client Paperwork

Using a real example, I accepted $3,000 worth of options in a six-person company called OnDisplay. Each share was worth .03 cents. This amount was declared and taxed that year. I had to take a gamble it was going to be worth anything at all, but given what I knew about the company, my own work on their behalf, and the small amount, I felt it was a smart business decision. The reason for paying taxes at the time of receipt is that it saves a lot of taxes if and when the firm has an exit event (purchased or going public).

In terms of sharing the options with each employee, **I determined the number of options the employees in my company would receive based on their time with the company and role.** The document was notarized, one copy given to the employee, while I retained the other. This protected both company and employee, in case I ever sold the business, died, or got into some other mess; the options would still be theirs.

When I accepted the first client stock options, it was just me and my first employee, my receptionist and all-around helper, a young woman of twenty-three with a college degree and eighteen months of work experience under her belt. She received about fifteen hundred options. When I added three more employees, options were provided and split among the entire team.

OnDisplay went public at $28.00 per share about three years later, and was purchased thereafter for over a billion dollars. The receptionist decided to pay off her college loans and had enough left over for a down payment on a house. A program manager chose to attend graduate school and take a trip to Europe.

If you are in the position of using stock options as an incentive for your employees, include a section that stipulates a timeframe for employment. In other words, **you don't want to give the options to the employee who decides to leave the following day**. Typical terms require the employee remain on board for at least one full year before the options are granted. The options are granted a quarter of the total amount per year, over four years. The options are forfeited if the employee decides to leave before the first year is up, or is terminated on grounds. This ensures that you, the owner, have loyalty of the employee for a solid twelve months.

> Be sure to keep the paperwork. One employee lost her documentation, and by the time I sent my copy and it was rectified, about sixty days were lost. Since she didn't have the stock certificate, the stock dropped after the profit-takers had their time. It eventually went back up, but she lost probably ten thousand dollars by misplacing her paperwork.

Using Milestone-Based Bonuses

Commissions should be distributed to those who contribute to a project, be it the receptionists, program managers, and consultants. **It's good for team building, since the entire group is supporting the closure of a client project, and it also can accelerate program completion.**

As the CEO, I did my best to include milestone-completion bonuses within the client engagement contract. This was used most often when the client had a particularly time-sensitive program and wanted to reward us for an early completion. **The other element of a project completion bonus would arise if we over-delivered.**

I'd seen how some public relations firms would get a bonus if their client received an appearance on the *Today Show* or in the *Wall Street Journal*. I wondered: Why can't this be applied to my business? From that time forward, if I could, I'd include an "over-deliver," clause. For example, if a licensing agreement was the program objective within a certain timeframe, but we closed a distribution and marketing agreement within the same time period (or shorter) as well, then a bonus was paid. This was either a flat fee or a percentage of the program value. Over time, I learned to make the payment a flat-fee, because the value was often hard to assess when the contract was signed, and wouldn't often produce results for three to six months. That left "the value" up for debate, which produced an angst-filled conversation. **Make it easy, use the flat fee approach for bonuses.**

As you share this money with your entire team, you'll have an invigorated, excited group of employees who will burst with creative ways to constantly over-deliver on projects. You will also have fewer defections to that same client, who will no doubt want to poach your outstanding, enthusiastic personnel.

These **bonuses also stimulate a sense of concern and caring about the client that lasts long after the paying engagement is complete**. Your team will likely keep tabs on the movements and growth of the client, changes in the market, and even new opportunities. I can recall reading a news article about a former client, having an idea or two about a possible partner development strategy, and then sending a quick e-mail off to the CEO, my point of contact. This unsolicited value was well received, even if the suggestion wasn't immediately enacted upon. Too often, I've heard clients say they feel a consultant will give them all the attention in the world as long as the checks are coming, but the minute that stops so does the contact.

Lunches and Getaways

If you think a great way to recruit employees is to explain profit sharing and bonus structures, imagine a prospective recruit's shock when you tell them that you also have company activities based on the success of the business. Before you stop reading, and argue that in an economic downturn people will be lucky to just have a job, I want to give you an example of how this approach pays off in the long-run.

Each January, I established revenue goals. Half-way through year three, the annual revenue goal was met, so I decided we had the extra funds to take a trip to Mexico with the employees' companion of choice. I told the team about it at a surprise lunch, where each employee at the company was handed a bag full of items necessary for a four-day tropical vacation.

When it came time to ask the employees to go the extra mile or to stay late, I found that I never had to get the words out. The employees just did it. **They were invested in the clients and the associated options or bonuses, but also because they felt a loyalty to me as the owner.** When your people see you sharing your good fortune with them, the investment pays off many times over.

Understandably, your consulting firm must be in good financial shape to support a $60 spa treatment or a Mexican vacation. Whatever form the reward takes, the result is a tremendous boost in morale and company goodwill.

When bad times hit: recognizing the signs

When the last economic downturn hit, the bank accounts and marketing budgets of businesses across all industries shrank. Our consulting revenue took a major dive over a period of six months, but I forged on, believing it was transitional and that our services would survive. **I should have realized we would continue to be a line item in the budget, but only if we adapted with the changing times**.

Here are the signs I should have seen, and what I should have done, (but didn't).

Uncommon Slowdowns

Typically, September-December are packed because many manufacturing companies launch new products. After a short lull, business picks up again in the spring, naturally heralded by the end of tax season. This intense schedule continued until the slowdown between July and August, then the cycle began again.

In comparing notes with other small business, I found that the majority also experienced this up-and-down cycle of fall and spring activity, late winter and late summer slowdown. **What I didn't notice was the difference between an uncommon (out of cycle) slowdown six months prior to the natural slowdown.**

It's a common saying that an economic slowdown will be felt by consultancies and small businesses six months before it is felt by the general population.

Looking back, I agree with that statement wholeheartedly. At that point, I should have seen the signs and re-assessed my business, our engagement focus, and the employees we had on staff.

Other indicators a recession or economic change is on the horizon include:

- ➢ High home costs (which are today, reaching 2008 levels)
- ➢ High debt (both the country and individual)
- ➢ Economic indicators such as mass retail and manufacturing layoffs, which have been occurring for the last eighteen months

If you see other economic indicators, perhaps now is the time to start adjusting your pricing structure. It's always better to prepare before the storm than when it's on the horizon. You could:

- ✓ Assesses your business model

- ✓ Reduce the scope and size of your offerings
- ✓ Piecemeal or separate out different services
- ✓ Evaluate staff or contractors

Change the Engagement Structure

I should have realized that methodologies were still important and necessary to our clients. I also should have adjusted faster, reducing the size, scope and cost because our offerings were out of budget for most companies hitting the downturn. The client could compromise while still achieving the business goal of increased revenue.

Unfortunately, I made a rookie mistake of adhering to the notion: "If it was going to be done, it was going to be done right." That's a great philosophy in times of plenty, but in lean times, do you know what the client will say? "It's got to be done *period*, and if you aren't going to modify the way you do business, we'll do it without you."

Not that these exact words were ever said to my face, but in hindsight, it was the essence of what occurred. I found myself losing business that three months earlier would have been a no brainer. I even went so far as to hold a five-day seminar in the Bay Area on partnerships hoping to attract new clients. That was a bust. While it was well attended, zero—and I mean zero—new clients came out of the effort. (Plus, it cost me twenty-five thousand dollars). It wasn't due to lack of content, as I was told. It was simply that our structure didn't match the time and requirement of the economy.

While this was happening, I continued paying out the salaries while the revenue slipped. That was the third mistake. I didn't adhere to my own rules about margins.

Never Break with Margins

The last and most crucial mistake I made regarding margins about did me in. Around month eight of the slump, I was looking at the cash flow, the money in the bank, and realized I was sixty days from being out of business. That didn't mean the doors were going to be shut, but the business "as I knew it" was going to change.

At this point, I recognized that the pricing structure was unsupportable and I immediately reduced the price of several proposals. This helped us win new business. The problem with that strategy was margins went down accordingly but my overhead costs associated with the full-time employees stayed the same. Now it became painfully clear to me why large companies use mass layoffs as a business strategy.

On this point, I ignored my accountant, who recommended either paring back employee compensation or reducing hours. Had I done either, layoffs probably would have been avoided. But no. I continued this course for yet another sixty days. In the end, I had to talk with my employees and provide the choice of letting them go or adjusting the employment arrangement, must as I'd been told to do.

Guess what? All but one employee (who decided to move out of state and get married), chose to take a change in status rather than leave the company. **Changing to a contractor status allowed me to retain the individuals and client consistency while eliminating entirely the overhead burden**. This was a proof point of creating employee loyalty I mentioned earlier.

Downsides of a Contractor

When my staff transitioned from full-time employees to contractors, the philosophy and loyalty to the company continued for several months, but I knew it wasn't going to last forever. The benefits, perks, and complete package they'd been used to, were too much to give up for most of the team members. I proactively let each employee know that if another opportunity arose, they were free to take it, no hard will. But if a contractor status was OK for the time being (or as long as the recession lasted), then the employment package for full-time employees would be reinstated as soon as it was feasible.

One by one, each one left to pursue other opportunities over the next nine months. But you know what? It was the best possible outcome, for it provided me the chance to hire contractors who had neither a requirement for a full benefits package nor expectations of revenue sharing.

Although contractors still needed to be excited about staying on past a single engagement, I modified the incentive structure to protect my own organization.

Version two of my incentive structure included the following:

Project fee: flat versus hourly. Having a specific payment schedule enabled me to offer the contractor an amount that met my margin requirements.

Commission for new projects. Rather than having a contractor scope out projects for himself or herself while working on my dime, I paid a fee ranging from seven percent to twelve percent as a commission for new business generated by the contractor. This kept my contractor motivated enough to refrain from getting greedy as interesting projects came along.

Pass-through bonus. When a project included a cash incentive for exceeding the goals, a percentage of the bonus was passed along to the contractor. I paid a straight forty percent of the bonus to the contractor who was the primary contributor, and sixty-five percent if the contractor was the end-to-end manager.

It may seem like a lot, but it's not. I'd already been paid on the original project and made a healthy margin. If I've been hands-off, relying on the expertise of the consultant who has performed beyond expectations, the bonus is well-deserved.

Milestone payments. Some contractors would like a monthly payment schedule, as it's better for cash-flow purposes. If the project is paid by dates, then it's possible.

Mike Konesky employed an automatic payment schedule based on milestone completion. With the milestone completed and signed off, an automatic invoice would be generated, then the invoice would be paid through wire transfer. No checks, no hassle, and no waiting for the contractor.

Non-competes. I had contractors sign a non-compete agreement, which is in effect for a period of twelve months after the last project is concluded. It's not a broad non-compete, preventing the contractor from doing any work. Instead, it's tailored to partner development. Of course, it's been pointed out time and again that non-competes are largely unenforceable (what small business wants to spend thousands of dollars going after a former employee or contractor) so it's mostly symbolic. Still, it identifies the conditions under which they are working for you, and certainly doesn't hurt.

Ten Consulting Vocations

Maybe you have volunteered at your church for twenty years and know quite a bit about establishing a new congregation, or you've managed social events at a retirement center. These are but two thriving consulting niches, for religion is never going away and neither are retirement centers.

1. **Church Operations Consultant**: consult church leadership on how to establish the best business systems for a smooth-running organization.
2. **Church Building Consultant**: consult churches on the best types of systems, music, prayer or sanctuary designs.
3. **Spiritual and Music Consultant**: consult churches on how to bring together music with a spiritual context for programs, worship, interactive newsletters and seminars.
4. **Computer Consultant**: consult churches on effective use of email systems, web pages, and donations.
5. **Church Event Consultant**: consult on aligning age appropriate events with themes, subject matter selection and speakers.
6. **Charity Fundraising**: consult with private entities about creating auctions, alumni programs and other types of fundraising programs, from setting the strategy to implementing and managing a fundraising program.

7. **Accreditation Consultant**: consult to new schools, private teaching entities that issue certifications, or professional continuing education on the requirements for accreditation.
8. **Curriculum Development Consultant**: consult to a specific type of school or corporate entity to develop curriculum, from a K-12 program to a software training course.
9. **Student Discipline Consultant**: consult to private or public schools on programs, tools, and methods to address a growing trend.
10. **Book Review Consultant**: consult to organizations about the books that their organization should include in their curriculum, or read and study for professional development. This could be subject matter focused, based on social, cultural, religious, ethnic or other persuasion.

Action items: Stage Seven

- ✓ Look to the future of your business: do you anticipate needing additional help, or would you prefer to constrain your business so you can do the work yourself?
- ✓ Visualize your client growth scenarios, adding in the type and number of staff you may require.
- ✓ Identify if the staff are contractor, part or full-time.
- ✓ Write out in detail, the skills associated with each staff member, along with realistic expectations (e.g. full-time requires full benefits etc.).

- ✓ Go back to your business model, typical client size (dollars) and the profit margin (revenue less expenses) and how much you can afford to pay the staff member.
- ✓ Evaluate the results: do you need to change a part of the business equation, e.g. raise the price of the service, modify the payment structure to the staff member, etc.
- ✓ If you can't afford average or typical salaries, consider other incentives that might interest potential staff members. Some health consultants can offer discounts on products, which can be worth more than cash, which will be taxed.
- ✓ Consider the use of non-compete or other tools that will lessen the possibility a contractor will leave.
- ✓ Initially, uses bonuses for projects completed early. As you become familiar with a staff member's interests, purchase a spa treatment, fishing gear or whatever makes financial sense. Those items are a tax deduction from the business and provide a great moral boost and decrease the chances your staff member will leave.

Hiring staff of any kind is an adventure, with certain complexities and advantages. Some consultants have found that the profit margin is far greater when the business is a sole proprietor, (not to mention easier to manager). Don't be surprised if you go down this path, only to change your mind later, maintaining a sole proprietorship.

I knew that if I failed I wouldn't regret that, but I knew the one thing I might regret is not trying.

Jeff Bezos, founder and CEO Amazon

Chapter Eight: Growing Your Business

To this point, we've touched on a few of the marketing and public relationships tools that can be used to tell people you are open and ready to be hired, from placing ads to speaking at events. In this chapter, I'm going to go another level down, focusing on the details.

The Written, Visual, and Audio Word

Dr. Satava's consulting business was a "direct result of speaking at industry forums," he told me time and again. Yet he was quick to acknowledge that the very reason he was invited to speak at those events was because he had written many papers on topics germane to his industry.

"I had to first take the time to sit and write on subjects that were important, yes, but established credibility for me in my field." In other words, being a surgeon wasn't enough. While he was still in college, Dr. Satava anticipated that being published was vital to his future work.

One doesn't need to be a surgeon to know that people (the average reader) places a certain amount of importance on the written word, be it a magazine, newspaper or book.

Polly Klein had tried events, but not as a speaker. If you recall from earlier chapters, she purchased a booth, spent a ton of money on expensive signage and walked away without a single client. It was only after she turned to writing for publications in her field did she gain the notoriety and eventual clients she so desired.

Writing is also a way to gain the national exposure you can't achieve through local (but still important) publications. With the advent of the Internet, blogging, YouTube and podcasting, consultants are no longer limited to writing for print media. Think of ways you can share your expertise with the masses, starting with some of the following proven outlets.

1. **Write for publications in your hometown**. Consider how you can differentiate yourself. As a landscape architect, can you become the expert known for sharing or promoting a unique or under-appreciated technique? Here are the steps:
   - Go to the library, a local restaurant or any "service" based business such as a doctor's office
   - Become familiar with all the publications, which usually range from real estate magazines to health, wellness, living and entertainment

- Write three different story ideas with 3-5 bullet points each
- Call or email the editor of the publication, pitch your idea(s) and what you bring that is different & unique as a contributor
- Provide a realistic date (or better yet, have all three written) and submit, along with photos (as they might not be able to send a photographer)

2. **Write for publications in your field.** Use the same approach but focus on your industry/area of work. Spend the time getting to know the publication(s).
   - Identify which section of the publication is best suited for your article (or opinion editorial)
   - Create a "pitch email" that includes three different components: 1) three short pitch ideas, 2) your unique qualifications (no more than a short paragraph) and 3) your flexibility/open mindedness about other topics not listed
   - Follow-up a week later if you don't hear back
3. **Write for complimentary industry publications**. A home-design consultant, such as a closet organizer, won't be the focus of a piece in a magazine focusing on remodeling. Yet a contributing, how-to piece on what to look for when designing or remodeling a home would be perfect.
   - Get educated on the last six issues of your ideal publication. Make sure you understand (and have perhaps

even written down) the articles that pertain to your line of work.

- Follow-the same approach as above, with the goal of being a contributing writer, and in the publication once or twice a year, on different topics.
- Consider alternative stories that include aspects of your work (office remodels and efficiency). Even if you start out as a single quote in a piece written by someone else, you have done two things. First, you have created a relationship with the editor (who told the reporter to include you as a source) and second, you have gotten your name out in the publication. This alone could give a boost to your business.

> **Reader time out:** Sometimes the editors are overwhelmed with offers of contributed articles. Don't let this stop you, just get creative. Using the above example, work with the builder or owner of the home/office where you worked. Sometimes the builder submits pictures of the home and has a pre-existing relationship with the editor. Conversely, a home owner will often be receptive to submitting their home for coverage in a publication. Be sure you are listed as a supplier or design element.

The moment the article is published, it's the start of your credentials. The piece can be re-used on your website and in other promotional materials, and referenced again and again as you pitch additional publications. "As seen in…." are three powerful marketing words. Use them.

- **Create a blog** and **link high-traffic sites**. Keep the content fresh and build a repository or archive or relevant pieces. Blogs are traditionally slow to gain readership but can accelerate your business revenue very quickly, especially if you sell products on your site. Incorporating a blog on your website is rather pointless unless you are actively directing people to the URL. Using other mechanisms to create this traffic, such as articles or radio, aids in gathering a following, while a blog satisfies the ongoing interest of those followers.

- **Provide expertise for the local radio**. Radio programs are dying for a fresh voice. Listen to the programs, identify where you can add value and interest to the listeners, and pitch the station on your credentials. **If the first program goes well, pitch the station manager or host on a regular spot.** Even a radio program with a modest audience, such as often found on AM stations, can be a tremendous boost to your credentials and another vehicle to accelerate your business.

- **Write a book**. If you are inclined to put your thoughts down in a larger format, then by all means, write a book. The benefits of having a book published on your chosen subject, can mean an incredible boost to your business and help to differentiate you from the competition.

Fast, easy and high impact

For consultants who have a finished manuscript but lack editorial and graphical services, both Amazon (through CreateSpace) and Barnes and Noble (through Nook Press) offer services for a fee.

Many consultants use books as a low-cost leader for selling higher-priced projects, and others who give their books to prospective clients. **On average, a printed book finds its way to the hands of seven readers.** This can be a great, low-cost selling tool because it will sit on the shelf of a client or prospect and is seen by others.

Get Involved

"Too many new business owners join the Chamber of Commerce or Rotary, give a business card and try to sell their services in the first conversation," said Bryan Kelley. He wasn't one of them. In fact, had it not been for a local economics professor, Bryan would never have even attended his first event, but he was glad he did.

"You don't get involved with the community business forums to make a quick buck. You do it because you are in it for the long haul." Today, Bryan looks back on his history with those two forums and says it took two or three years for his firm to financially benefit.

"The head of the Chamber was my direct competitor, so I had to tread lightly." It was a good thing though, because Bryan wanted his reputation to do the talking, not him. "My business is one that's all about trust. If you are in the community and active, and they like who you are, they will send business your way. If they think you are a pompous prick, you are screwed."

Bryan's advice for the new business owner is to the point. "Don't go in and talk about your business, other than to name it. Gather knowledge, understand the initiatives and build trust. Eventually, the business will come."

Bryan has always tried to track where his referrals come from, and he estimates that at least 8-15% of his annual business is directly related to someone at the Chamber of Commerce or the Rotary.

"It's the soft sell and it's the long play," he says, but being involved also pays dividends in other way.

"If you are a business that's truly struggling—and every small business struggles at some point—it's very rare that you can't knock on the door and buy them a lunch in return for some advice. Chances are, they have faced the same struggles and it comes down to leadership".

The small business that succeeds is run by the owner who can ask a question when he or she needs help.

Bryan Kelley

Productizing Your Business

Consulting can be profitable, but **the goal of many consultants is to somehow productize the business so money can be made 24:7, 365 days a year.** The whole foods consultant will create a line of healthy creams. The remodeling expert will create a podcast and charge a dollar. The retail consultant (or even employee) will create a line of socks. The commonality is products are sold any time of the day or night and are not limited to being sold in a traditional retail channel, thanks to Internet sales.

> The goal of most consultants is to somehow package the service offering (made up of his or her own intellectual capital) in a way that can be shipped and sold as easily as a toothbrush or downloadable application. This is called productizing your service, and allows mass quantities of a single product to be sold again and again without your hands-on intervention.

Productization of services can take many forms and run the gamut of price points and sophistication. You might even find that productizing your knowledge is more profitable (and easier) than an actual consulting practice (which you may decide to phase out).

Create a Product Kit

Let's use the example of a landscape consultant who creates a plan for a client, then refers that client to the local nursery to purchase products, or to a store to buy books to gather ideas. This same landscape consultant could create a first-time home buyer's "get-started kit" that can be sold for $19.95 on the Internet.

As a reader of landscaping books and magazines myself, I can attest to finding one or two interesting ideas per book before becoming frustrated at the lack of details. My next stop is the library or other landscape shops. This adds to the cost of the entire project, and I haven't even started doing any work.

For many products, I'm like the average consumer. I'll spend the money for a big project, but for all the day-to-day items, I'm going to try the do-it-myself approach. I would turn to an easy-to-use, detail-filled product in a heartbeat.

In my perfect world, a landscape kit would include detailed and comprehensive documents, all electronic and downloadable, ready to use and easily modified. One document could be a spreadsheets of a PDF of landscape illustrations and colored diagrams with plants. A second electronic document might be a spreadsheet with a timeline of what needs to be accomplished by what time of year. A third electronic document could be an itemized listing of all the necessary items required to create the landscape.

Now you might ask, "Why would I purchase this package, since the local Home Depot has books, the local landscaping company has a checklist, and the local hardware store has all the items I need?"

The answer boils down to differentiation, convenience, and cost. A book requires waiting for it to arrive. Most reference books are purchased in hard copy form or I must go to the store and get it, whereas I could purchase and download a kit in the middle of the night wearing my pajamas, printing out the information and getting started on my own schedule.

Product sales are an immediate way for a prospective client to first review and test your theories and expertise before spending a lot more money with your services. Furthermore, with your credibility established (by virtue of having a Kit available for sale), potential clients can see your work and contact you directly for your services.

If you have used the earlier process regarding staged marketing, then you likely have a website established, you may have a newsletter, and are blogging about your area of expertise. Up to now, these marketing vehicles have provided prospects with only one option: your consulting services. Now you provide two options; services and products.

Just as exciting should be the ability to go back and blog to promote your new product line. This is worthy of a press release, sidebar articles, and even radio airtime. Just be sure to mention where consumers can purchase the products.

Starter Productization Checklist

1. Review the products on the market in your area of expertise.
2. Determine whether you can compile your knowledge and expertise in a written set of materials, presented in a "how-to" format.
3. Validate how your products are unique and compelling.
4. Write the list of the items to be in your kit, then actually create each one. You may already be using each of the documents in your business, so repurposing the documents, spreadsheets, presentations, or who knows what else, may be fast and easy.
5. Remove confidential information that might be included in your materials so it can be used for the masses.
6. Prepare it for electronic distribution and have it ready to distribute.
7. Create the product page(s) and establish the payment system.

8. Strongly consider establishing a PayPal merchant account if you don't already have one.
9. Create the Purchase button (a simple step-by-step process), and cut and paste this information in to your website. Once done, the PayPal logo will appear, and you will be ready to sell the product on your website.
10. Promote and link the new kit on your landing (home) page, as well as other blogs and materials you are writing.
11. Send out an announcement to former clients, with something like "If you have always wanted to do [insert your expertise here], but couldn't afford the time or money, you now have the opportunity through this great [insert expertise here] kit that's now available through [you, your firm, or other branded company]."
12. Consider placing this in a newsletter.
13. Support your new (no-cost products) with on-line ads. Consider Google Ads, Yahoo! or a host of other on-line providers, depending on your personal preference.

Premium Products

Jim Robb started in sales twenty-five years ago and gradually expanded into all facets of corporate leadership, including new business development, marketing, and capital acquisition. Seven years ago, he formed The ROBB Group, a consultancy located in Scottsdale, Arizona. With Robb's background, he naturally founded the firm to focus on revenue acceleration through sales and business-development advisory services and products.

Jim eventually hired Mark Dallmeier as his CEO, who brought methodologies and best practices for accelerating revenue growth to his firm. One of his first tasks was to quickly transfer Jim's successful revenue generation methods to do-it yourself revenue-acceleration products. Mark believed the real power of revenue acceleration was to be found in self-managed products that could be used by the client at their own location long after the consultants work was finished.

The first product was a business-assessment form that prospects completed on-line. The purpose of the free assessment was two-fold: benchmark the current state of performance and revenue generation or growth through the company's existing models, methods, practices, personnel, while identifying the strengths and weaknesses of the prospect for their own benefit.

The results of the questionnaire provided a metric of comparatives that identified how well the answers fared against the performance of similar companies. The questionnaire covered the primary company areas of marketing, sales, partner and business development, and vision and goals tying together internal and marketplace dependencies that were inhibiting revenue growth.

Other assessments would evolve to include the gathering of competitive analysis and intelligence, leadership and employee skills, behaviors, motivators and experience. The resulting outcomes identified urgent business strategy, process optimization and transformation requirements of the company if it was to enter or sustain double digit organic revenue growth. This informed client executives of the revenue at risk and the revenue opportunity that could be captured by evolving or transforming the business' strategy or its sales and marketing models.

According to Jim , business assessments typically run between several thousand to over fifty thousand dollars, depending on the depth and scope. As an executive, he'd hired many firms to provide this service, and believed it would be a tremendous way to provide immediate value at no cost to the prospect.

"This would graduate to a larger, more strategic consulting projects," he reasoned.

All told, initial development of the first assessment product line was roughly six months and approximately $20,000. **Instead of paying the $20,000 cash for product development, he provided a percentage of ownership in the product line to his main software developer**. In terms of hard-dollar cost, Jim incurred operational costs associated with an office and telephone lines and the like, line items already budgeted for the consulting business.

Jim and Mark's initial belief that the assessment would bring more consulting projects was accurate. What surprised both of them was the extent to which the on-line assessment could be leveraged in to a whole line of sales-acceleration products.

As the products proved successful, Jim and Mark quickly moved to extend the line outside strictly sales, each time pausing long enough to test out the product with consumers and gain customer success stories and metrics before moving to the next product. **Additional products were developed through customer engagements and testing to provide an end to end offering that would drive immediate revenue growth and results.** These products include best practice methods and tools for quantifying how a company's target customer buys and makes purchasing decisions, to process and practices for validating a company's unique value proposition, and methods for establishing a differentiated sale and go to market model.

"By understanding how a company's target customer buys and makes decisions, you can optimize the selling process and package it into steps for strategic selling to an electronic format, so even the most junior sales executive can ramp up quickly, using a proven format," explained Mark Dallmeier, the ROBB Group's CEO. "Most companies fail in the sales area by leaving too much up to the individual rep or manager without supporting those individuals through an updated, modern sales system, process and set of resources."

As their learning grew, the ROBB Group continued to develop more products to meet the training and education needs of their clients.

Testing and Proving Product Worth

The ROBB Group proved the value of their assessment by packaging it and providing it for free, gaining valuable intelligence, including quotes and input from prospects and former clients alike. **The most important elements were the metrics** identifying things such as shortened sales cycles, increased transaction volume and average dollar amount per sales, improved margin, reduction of product returns, and improved customer satisfaction.

A great example of a customer quote is from the vice president of sales at MCI.

After four months of dealing with a stalled outsourcing deal, the ROBB Group helped us develop a pursuit plan...we received the $100,000,000 memorandum of understanding within three weeks after their help.

Vice President, MCI

The Enterprise Integration Group responsible for global outsourcing agreements at MCI (eventually Verizon Business) grew from $300 million in revenues to over $1.6 billion in revenues within a span of 24 months while utilizing The ROBB Group assessments, methods, and sales support experts within its major accounts. As soon as Jim and Mark saw customer trends around types of sales issues, they developed additional methods, practices and product lines.

One of the considerations for extending a product line was the customer feedback. Jim's initial on-line assessment product evolved to four different audits: one for sales, another for a sales pipeline audit, a channel growth audit, and a final marketing differentiation audit. These individual products were enhanced to include detailed recommendations, process changes, models, and methods to improve the organizational output.

Jim and Mark put an emphasis on getting quotes after every client engagement, usually within fifteen days of project completion. One such quote is the following: "The ROBB Group completed Revenue Recovery Audits and provided our teams methods, processes and resources that made our vision and growth objectives operational within 45 days, enabling us to reduce sales cycles and costs while increasing our average transaction sizes by 75% — strategically repositioning the company and sales team with C level clients and prospects." CEO, Cybermetrics.

They used quotes like this to take the consulting firm to an ever-larger audience. They plan to evolve and elevate these often overlooked and underserved professionals by embedding their unique methods, practices, and products into a global society of professionals that hunt revenue, eventually providing much needed certification and mentoring to over 30 million sales professionals worldwide. With the incredible quotes this firm generates, and a stable of brand-name clients, it is applying the expert role to an industry thought leader, driving a new type of thinking about a way of doing business—in this case, selling to large companies.

It should be noted that The ROBB Group has two employees: the CEO Mark Dallmeier and the founder, Jim Robb. Their small business will periodically hire a contractor, but for most engagements, it's just the two of them.

There are two kinds of experts; practical experts and academic experts. One is not better than the other, but they are very different, and add very different value.

Simon Sinek

How is an expert defined?

Over the years, I watched lawyers, consultants, former generals and just about anyone else, including businessmen and women from all sorts of fields, giving "expert opinions" and advice on CNN. Were they really experts in their fields, with multiple degrees, pedigrees of successful clients or projects three decades long, or were they little more than good-looking, articulate professionals capable of conjuring pithy, ten-second sound bites?

Beyond four-star military generals, I've come to believe that the experts I see on TV are no better than most of the other working professionals in a given field. **The only difference is that those featured on television possess the ability to promote themselves in a way that differentiates them from the competition.** On top of this, the expert is available at the odd times of the day or night required by the media.

Without a doubt, creating and leveraging the title of expert is one of the fastest ways to gain new clients, along with continuing positive media coverage. And for a person to achieve the expert designation, it is important to have a few credentials already established. In the medical or legal field, credentials are your licensed status. Architects are constantly referred to by their latest project and movie producers are known by their latest success (or failure).

In the business world, credentials are as much about whom you have worked with as how the facts are presented.

You have now read about establishing credentials through written articles, being quoted on the air or in print, and then of course, your own projects. These lend to your status as an expert, a phrase that you can use to accelerate your business.

Bryan Kelley is considered an expert, and it wasn't an age that made him so, he was likely an expert in his early twenties, but his work resume would be considered thin.

"It wasn't until after I'd owned my business and became involved in the industry associations and the local business forums that I started to hear my name and the term expert in the same sentence."

Polly Klein and Becky Bishop both work with animals but their work is totally different. Yet, both women have risen to the top of their respective fields and have been designated as experts.

Becky Bishop gained the expert status when she won awards for her puppy-training program. After she started group classes, she got her name into several competitions and was profiled by local magazines. Shortly thereafter, she was named Best Bet for your Pet by *Seattle Magazine* and for two years was named "Best in the Northwest" by *City Dog Magazine*. Not bad, considering that the dog training competition is fierce, including the pet giant PetSmart. Polly Klein, on the other hand, attained expert status after first writing articles, teaching at a university, and being the subject of numerous profiles in television segments and print coverage in major publications, where she was referred to as an expert.

You've read how Dr. Satava first wrote in journals, which led to the speaking opportunities, which created his consulting businesses.

"It's a circular effort that continues to build upon itself," he said. "The more I know about the government, technology or private sectors, the more I'm asked to speak, the more clients I get."

The only downside to being an in-demand expert, Dr. Satava cautions, is a very busy travel schedule.

"Three days a week, I'm at my office at the Pentagon, in Virginia. I fly out Wednesday night, have a clinic on Thursday, and surgery on Friday."

He likes to be busy by nature and enjoys the extra income, which is anywhere from fifty to sixty thousand in a year, more than enough for him to continue his hectic schedule. "This is on top of my salary from the University where I'm is employed full-time." Gaining the expert status and leveraging it from one area to another have afforded him a very good second (or third) income.

"I love being a consultant, but more than that, I love learning. It keeps every day fresh and unique."

My biggest motivation? Just to keep challenging myself. I see life almost like one long University education that I never had — every day I'm learning something new.

Richard Branson, founder Virgin Group

Public events, private engagements and more clients

In Seattle, I spoke at several events designed specifically for entrepreneurs and small business owners. The Business Journal monthly breakfast meeting was one, another was the Entrepreneur Organization. Both were done free of charge, lasted an hour, and had attendees of 200-400 people. Following both, I was contacted by venture capital firms. Some wanted me to speak to their partners while others asked me to address their portfolio companies. Those were closed-door, invitation only events, with fewer than twenty persons at each. From just two events I gained four new clients.

Bryan Kelley's comment about taking the long view doesn't apply just to the Chamber of Commerce, but every opportunity where you, the consultant, have a light to shine upon others who may know of others who will eventually pay you for your knowledge.

Retired, then not

At one of these venture capital meetings, I met a man who was an investor and advisor. As I asked about his background, I was humored by the fact he called himself a consultant, and lasted about a year in retirement. He got bored, but didn't want to be employed and have a boss, so he put out the word he was available for hire.

He had worked with all the major automobile manufacturers as a manager then a senior executive and wanted to consult in his area of expertise. Rather than consult for "the big guys," he'd chosen to consult to those small entities as an "executive-on-call." This married his passion for the industry with a love of assisting parts suppliers working with the big automotive players.

When he started, many of his past contacts had either retired or were in a different part of the business that didn't apply to his area of interest. **He needed to start over and decided to do so by focusing on getting in front of a new audience through events and conferences**. He targeted only forums directed at small parts manufacturers, positioning himself as an expert in the field.

"It only took me one event to start conversations with a half-dozen companies and two turned into clients that month. Another came on as a part-time retainer relationship the following month."

The goal wasn't money, although "it was good," he said. He wanted to be in the game and "help other small business owners who were just starting out and needed a leg up."

Reader time out: Have you been requested to provide a gardening seminar at the local Home Depot or boutique nursery? If you are a landscaping consultant in the northwest, you can barely walk five feet without running into your competition. Even serving as a guest educator at a local nursery can be the start of creating an expert status while gaining new clientele. This one-time guest educator role can be turned in to a guest expert spot on a local radio station, and this in turn can generate additional clientele. The goal is to create an immediate point of differentiation from your competition. The number of times, locations, and prestige of the organizations that rely upon your advice will accelerate your status, and your business revenue.

Ten Consulting Vocations

Did you sell golf clubs as a teenager and software after graduating from college? Perhaps you are good at networking and organizing groups where others meet up and create business relationships. Each one of these skills opens the door to a consulting practice.

1. **Business Networking Consultant**: consult clients on how to create a networking forum to increase revenue.
2. **Business Capture Consultant**: consult with clients to improve revenue through new sales and business development strategies across industries and regions.
3. **Contract Consultant**: consult to clients on specific deal negotiation, business planning and marketing.
4. **Acquisition Consultant**: consult with clients who are undertaking mergers, acquisitions, and divestitures.
5. **Home-based Consultant**: consult with individuals who want to start a home-based business and need assistance in getting started, getting marketed, and closing sales.
6. **Animal Communicator Consultant**: consult with pet owners, veterinarians, and animal clinics on hard to manage animals.
7. **Relocation Consultant**: if you have been in human resources and specialized in relocation packages, or the actual logistics of relocation, you can consult to small, medium, or large companies on bettering their relocation partners, packages, or processes.
8. **Revenue Accelerator Consultant**: consult to mid or large size businesses on strategies and programs to dramatically improve revenue generation.
9. **Recreational Business Development Consultant**: consult to spas, resorts, golf clubs or other recreationally-centered business on

programs designed to increase revenue per event, per service or per stay.

10. **Government Business Development Consultant**:

    consult to a foreign government's trade commission (e.g. Canada) on programs to improve trade to that country.

Action Items: Stage Eight

- ✓ Evaluate the necessity and value of becoming a recognized expert in your community or on a national level.
- ✓ Consider the most cost-effective, high-impact ways to get started—is it through getting to know the local editors, radio producers or event sponsors?
- ✓ Pitch the appropriate contact person for submitting an article or being a guest on a show.
- ✓ Encourage the relationship to the point where you are a regular contributor or are the "go-to" person for that subject.
- ✓ Leverage your local expert status to a national level if this will help your business and reputation.
- ✓ Consider the possibility of adapting your knowledge and know-how to a product that can be sold or given away.
- ✓ Look at all possible options for collecting and packaging a how-to kit, from documents to an on-line product assessment.
- ✓ Evaluate the best format for your products as well as the cost and possible return on investment.

- ✓ Validate the need with your target customers (and/or existing clients), gain feedback, and then leverage the input for marketing purposes
- ✓ Use the products as giveaways and promotional tools to extend the awareness and visibility of the product line

CHAPTER

If your business partners aren't working as hard as you, it's not a partnership. It's a sinking ship.

Julian Hall

Chapter Nine: Partnering for Success

Smart partnerships accelerate the growth of a company, bring new products to market, open new referral and distribution channels, and even lower the cost of goods sold. For consultants, partnerships should be considered throughout the lifecycle of the business.

As a consultant, you need to know that partnerships are, and will be, an important element of a corporate strategy, and the type of partnership generally depends on the stage of your company.

For instance, Becky Bishop is no partner expert, as she will tell you. But she employed a common sense approach to create a formal network of referrals among her competitors.

"I actually asked a few dog-training facilities if they would refer to me for in-home puppy help, since they didn't offer the service, and that flopped," said Becky. "The well-established facilities sort of just patted me on the head, and told me, 'Good luck!' She never did get a referral from them. So, she got creative and networked with other trainers in the area. **She formed a triangle among three companies who only refer to each other**. Becky believed that enough clients exist for all three organizations and that if she may as well keep them in the family and send them to the trainer she networks with.

The business motivation behind creating a partnership is to dramatically accelerate revenue at a fraction of the cost. It is a rare that one partnership fits all, since companies mature and can outgrow a partnership.

A partnership could include co-marketing your products and services, like the kind exemplified by the attorney and insurance company owner who held seminars at the local library. Consultants can choose to create products, license, sell and distribute these products (along with their services) jointly or separating, giving one another a share of the revenue.

Companies of all sizes, and under any economic conditions, will always be looking for partners for a simple reason: It's hard to survive without them.

Know Your Goals

When I decided to partner with Hunt Interactive to develop my line of products (which have seen been merged with another company, and are no longer available as stand-alone products), I did so with very clear partnership goals:

- Get my products created with the least amount of money; and

- Ensure that the products could live on the Internet without a large investment of time and money on my part.

Hunt's capabilities addressed both goals, as they had the software to assist in creating the products, as well as the server capacity to handle thousands of concurrent users of the product line. In return for finding a partner willing to help me achieve my goals, I willingly gave up a part of the revenue.

I'll provide another, more recent example. One of my passions is writing fiction, although passion doesn't always translate to getting a mainstream publisher. And unlike the patience I displayed when working with McGraw-Hill for my first trade book, I was unwilling to wait another two to three years for my debut fiction book to come to market.

The only way I could do it myself was to partner with a designer to create the cover art and inside illustrations. At the time, a custom cover would have cost thousands of dollars, so I offered the illustrator a revenue-sharing deal of $.50 per book, regardless of quantity. He took more risk, but his upside was high. He made $3,000 in the first few months after the book went on sale, and used that as spending money for an overseas trip with his wife.

The difference from a 'trade' is that I had nothing to trade in return for the cover art. We became partners when this illustrator accepted a portion of the back-end revenue for the service he was providing up front. He had to take the risk I was a) going to complete the book and b) the book was going to sell enough to cover his costs and maybe a little more. For my part, I had to convince him of both those things, neither which were guarantees. Because of this, my offer of fifty cents per book was far above what is considered normal in the publishing industry, which is either a flat fee (and zero back end) or a more modest fee of ten cents ($.10).

Common Customers

Consider the consulting firm Appalachian Partners, (www.appalachianresources.com), based in Rose Hill, Virginia. Appalachian Partners provides management and fundraising consulting services to non-profits. This field is packed, and growing larger by the day as consultants attempt to satisfy the demand of more and more non-profits across the country. Appalachian Partners has a long list of clients, including Virginia Commonwealth University, Appalachian School of Law, and Emory & Henry College.

Like the industry it serves, Appalachian Partners has segmented its target market according to specific niches, including education and arts. To serve its client base better, Appalachian has partnered with organizations offering specific grants to specific industry sectors. The marketing partnership includes listing the other organization on its website (under Hot Funding Opportunities), with a summary of the grant program. Details about the grant are included, along with the direct e-mail address and URL.

The visitor to the site, or grant seeker, isn't required to use Appalachian at all. **The entire purpose behind the marketing partnership is to provide value to the visitor up front**. Then, if and when the visitor or grant seeker gets stuck in the grant process, Appalachian might be the choice to provide actual services.

In return for providing the grant opportunity on the Appalachian website, the providers of the grant link back, list or do both, for Appalachian on their Resources page.

The demographic of both entities is the same (the individual or firm looking for the grant), and the marketing partnership provides both the consulting organization and the grant provider a no-cost means of creating awareness of, and demand for, this target market. Marketing partnerships are often low- or no-cost efforts and can provide the air under your consulting business's wings.

A marketing partnership: When two companies refer business, or potential clients to one another.

A sales partnership: When a commission is provided to one or both parties when a sale is made. In other words, money changes hands.

Once you have assessed the target demographic, you are ready to identify and select specific organizations. The easiest way to do this is to create your target customer's *Circle of Influence*. In this model[4], your target client is placed in the center of a circle, and the complimentary service or product offers are placed around the center. Begin with the most basic of necessities that define the target client.

---

[4] Detailed and described in Navigating the Partnership Maze: Creating Alliances that Work, McGraw-Hill

Your target client:

- Shops (mall, boutiques, on-line, mail order)
- Drives/Rides (cars by type, rides a bike, commutes via public transportation)
- Lives (apartment, condominium, townhouse, high-rise, home; urban or suburban)
- Banks (remotely, in-store)
- Eats (at home, in restaurants)
- Wears (casual, custom, low-end clothing)
- Travels (in-state, by recreational vehicle, flies overseas, domestic)
- Sleeps (at home, on planes, away from home)
- Plays (extreme sports, outdoor activities by type)
- Pets (horses, dogs, cats)
- Enjoys hobbies (lifestyle activities, flying, scrap-booking)
- Believes (in religion, conserving nature)

For this exercise, be as specific as possible in the category surrounding your target client. You will be surprised exactly how much you know about your target client, especially if your business is geared toward consumers rather than businesses, although the exercise is equally valuable. After you complete this exercise, you will be ready to assign actual brand names beside each category.

For example:

- Shops (on-line: Amazon, eBay, GI Joe's, Nordstrom)
- Wears (Gap clothes, Swiss Army watches)
- Travels (in RV on the weekends)
- Has (dogs)

With this information, you are assembling the potential partners for your business. In the beginning, you can name as many brands or entities as possible. To create partnerships, however, you need to reduce this to a manageable number, perhaps three or five organizations. Do so by identifying organizations that are local to you, or those with whom you have an existing relationship. Now you are ready to consider your pitch and the goals of the partnership.

Complimentary Offerings

Partnerships can result in referrals received through web site links or off-line referrals from a local hardware store where you gave a seminar, or a combination of the two. No rules exist for a complimentary partner, other than that the outcome should result in revenue.

Consider one example of a bridal consultant and an event management firm. In this case, it's a traditional partnership resulting in new leads, new clients, and additional revenue.

Bridal consulting is a fascinating consulting niche, and not just because it deserves its own Bravo reality show. **Bridal consulting**

generates hundreds of millions of dollars a year, and has literally no barrier to entry. One day, a seamstress can be making bridal dresses in the backroom and the next day can be consulting to Macy's or Bloomingdale's. From accessories to custom-made products to retailers and wholesalers, the list of niches within bridal consulting is like the colors of the rainbow. That's why it's such a great example for consultants in other areas of apparel or retail: So many partnership opportunities exist.

Here's one scenario.

A bridal consultant in the northeast wants to accelerate her business, so she creates a Circle of Influence and soon realizes that a local event-management company handles most of the weddings. After some investigation, she learns that the hotels, wineries, and nice restaurants already have in-house bridal consultants. Even so, she's not disheartened because she realizes that local travel companies (service-provider consultants) want to increase their revenue through local packages they can offer tourists. This bridal consultant then learns the smaller wineries and bed and breakfasts lack the funds to staff full-time bridal consultants but would love to tap into this market space.

The bridal consultant identifies a potential market niche, assisting the local food and beverage companies as well as the destination hotspots. They are interested but concerned that the bridal consultant is a one-person organization, without the benefit of a staff, should a large wedding get booked.

Her first step is to pitch the event-management company on expanding into a new market niche, but one that is far less lucrative than their traditional business. Not only are they interested in her business offering, they are extending their own line of business into in-store bridal fashion shows.

The marketing partnership begins with the event-management company gaining the contract for a large department store bridal fashion show. The bridal consultant provides her services for free, working with the department store and other vendors in return for free marketing and promotion. The result is that prospective clients (brides-to-be) sitting in the audience, request a bridal consultant. She gets a new client, and because she agrees to use the dresses from the department store (if required), the hosting store of the bridal event benefits. The event-management company is recommended for the wedding (although the final choice is up to the bride), and of course, the bridal consultant gains a new client in the process.

At the same time, the bridal consultant leverages the reputation of her event-management partner by jointly presenting their services to the local food and beverage firms and destination locations. With an established, reputable firm as her partner, the bridal consultant closes the sale, and has the flexibility to bring in the event management partner as necessary.

This is a simple example of a traditional partnership that yields a lucrative revenue stream for each organization involved. The out-of-pocket costs for the consultant are limited to time and travel costs.

But even on this note, the fee is negotiable. The consultant need not provide time for free, but that may be necessary to get a foot in the door at the event management firms and establish a relationship.

In another example, a jewelry maker is also known as a bridal jewelry consultant, making custom headbands and clips, desires to increase revenue through partnerships. The strategy is to partner with existing entities (or other consultants) that offer jewelry to an established customer base.

Princessbands (www.princessbands.com) is one such entity that holds jewelry parties for bridal showers, but also sweet sixteen parties, girls nights out, and even jewelry-making parties.

One way to extend her own venue is to partner with a sales consultant in a complimentary area, from sterling silver jewelry to lingerie and other types of clothing or from honeymoon wear to home products. These Multi-Level Marketing (MLM) niches are among the fastest-growing and most profitable in the country.

Enter the MLM consultant. This is an example of a mixed partnership, where one entity sells on-line but can also sell offline (in person, in a traditional venue) to and through partners.

The goal of the partnership is to dramatically extend the visibility of the custom jewelry line with little or no out-of-pocket expense. In kind, the MLM salesperson is always on the scout for venues to display their goods and present to new customers. The result is that a complimentary demographic benefits the new customers of each organization. The payback is new revenue for the MLM consultant as well as for Princessbands. Here again, the marketing and promotion is a low- or no-cost means to create awareness and immediate revenue.

Contracts

Not all partnerships require a formal, signed contract. **Contracts become important when revenue is being created, and money is changing hands.**

Referrals are considered a component of a marketing partnership, the least formal type of partnerships and rarely require a signed agreement. Not all consultants have Becky Bishop's good fortune of being referred by veterinarians who are helping out stressed-out new dog owners. For all other types of partnerships based on generating money, it's good to have an agreement in place.

- **Marketing partnership**: Used when referrals result in a product or service sales. A formal referral program might include providing the partner with an accounting of new business, the source of the business, the dollar amount of the transaction, and a percentage of the revenue (gross, not net) for the referral fee. If you're uncomfortable providing your partner with a gross revenue number, then use a flat referral fee.
- **Distribution partnership**: Used when your partner is distributing your products or services, or you are distributing your partner's products or services. E.g. you supply the remodeling consulting and they supply landscape consulting). If you provide a well-qualified lead that turns into a sale, you should pay the consultant 10% to 20% of the fee for the referral.
- **Licensing partnership**: Used when you are licensing a product from another company and reselling it with your own services. You may or may not attach your own name to this agreement. A great example is a non-profit consultant that licensed a type of process for gaining educational grants from a professor. The non-profit consultant pays the professor an annual fee for the usage of this process in return for invisibly incorporating the process into his own business.

- **Joint development partnership**: In this scenario, you and the other entity are jointly developing a new product or service and are going to share in the ownership and/or revenue from the resulting asset. It's vitally important to clearly delineate the asset created, the ownership, profits and losses, liability, and the terms of the revenue receipt and payment.

Partner Pitfalls

Not all partner experiences are going to turn out well. Yet, you can limit the potential problems by becoming familiar with the mistakes consultants commonly make when crafting a new partnership.

The number-one pitfall is the lack of clarity around the objectives for each organization. You may want to increase revenue in thirty days, while your partner might not care about doing so for three to six months. Worse, you can have several conversations about the requirement for revenue, but with different expectations, the partnership is doomed to fail.

Another pitfall is lack of communication among partners. Read any blog on partnerships, be it between consultants or manufacturing companies, and you will read the same thing: the lack of communication between the partners leads to a broken partnership.

Communication is as simple as checking in once a week to tell one another about the state of referrals, new clients, upcoming events, and, most importantly, what you are doing to increase revenue (or meet the stated objectives of the partnership). In return, you should be receiving this type of information back from your partner.

You can keep this pitfall at arm's length by brainstorming with your partner about an event, upcoming campaign, or program that continually infuses new energy and excitement into the effort.

Beyond giving the team a goal to work towards, deadlines force activity. With client engagements, pitching new prospects or even paying bills, it can be hard to re-focus on a partnership. Be careful to pay attention! Partnerships can sustain a business in lean times, and accelerate it during times of plenty. However, a partnership will yield nothing if it's not pruned on a weekly basis.

Breaking the Partnership

Ending a partnership doesn't have to be acrimonious. **The key to avoiding a lot of bad feelings is to have a well-thought-out plan in the beginning**, and put forth the objectives and desired outcomes in writing. This doesn't mean a partnership requires a signed, notarized document. In many cases, even an e-mail thread is enough to remind both parties of the original intent of the partnership. A document of this type serves as the baseline from which to gauge the situation, and the remedy (or termination) of the partnership.

The smart partnership expert will anticipate a break-up and include necessary terms in the original document. For instance:

- Who owns the client list (one or both parties)?
- What is the term of the deal? In other words, for all leads generated and sales that occurred, how long with referrals, commissions or fees be paid? The term, or time frame, during

which you will get paid after the end of a partnership can last from thirty days to six months or a year.

- What is the policy for future referrals from an existing client?
- What is the non-compete policy, or a non-competing partnership? In this case, a firm is required to use the same organization for a period of time, or provide a service themselves rather than partner with a competitor.
- Upon partnership termination, which entity is responsible for outstanding guarantees or warranties made to the client?
- What happens to the partnership if one entity is sold, merges with another firm, or goes out of business?

This happened during the time I had a partnership with Hunt Interactive. A much larger firm acquired Hunt, and my software database products were on still on the Hunt Interactive servers. Furthermore, the revenue-sharing deal could have been null and void with sale, but neither I nor the CEO of Hunt, John Hunt, had thought to place this in the documentation.

Fortunately, we hammered this out in a single, simple conversation, with Hunt agreeing to transfer hosting of my products to a new entity without charge. We mutually decided to terminate the revenue-sharing agreement due to the acquisition.

Not all partnership endings are so easy. I learned from this, and from that point on, I included terms for a partnership break due to an acquisition, in every agreement.

Ten Consulting Vocations

Did you coordinate engagements, conduct research or create programs for your previous employer? Have you ever edited your roommate's papers in college for free pizza? Do you enjoy reading so much that you edit manuscripts after you finish your day job at the law firm?

1. **Skills Development Consultant**: consult with preschools, teachers, parents and community centers on programs for youth, teens and the elderly to continue skills development.
2. **Contemporary Programs Consultant**; consult with retirement centers, church groups, non-profits and other facilities caring for the elderly about programs to encourage activity and stimulation.
3. **Outreach Consultant**: consult with youth centers and for-profit corporations to create mentoring programs.
4. **Community Center Consultant**: consult with community centers about how to better work with entities that offer technical services, physical programs and even intellectual programs to partner for the good of the community.
5. **Corporate Events Consultant**: consult with corporate clients and their event staffs on the best programs for team building, conflict resolution and other goals that improve the community and give back in a meaningful way.
6. **Bridal Consultant**: consult in one of a hundred areas for the bridal industry that is specific to your area of interest, location and special knowledge you might have.

7. **Jewelry Consultant**: consult your clients on how to better sell their product to jewelry buyers, creators or distributors to improve revenue.
8. **Swim Instruction Consultant**: consult with individual, community or local pools on creating programs for all types of age groups and demographics, suited for specific communities.
9. **Travel and Destination Consultant**: consult to local wineries, bed and breakfast establishments or unique destinations on how to increase regional and national awareness and demand to improve revenue.
10. **Special Events Consultant**: consult with small destination entities that can't afford a full-time internal events manager.

Action Items: Stage Nine

- ✓ Consider the organizations in your community who serve your ideal client.
- ✓ Determine if any of those entities are presently working with your competitor, or a service provider similar to yourself.
- ✓ If you have run out of ideas for potential partners, use the Circle of Influence to identify the categories of products and services used by your target client. Add in the local providers of some of those products and services.
- ✓ Prioritize by local entities or those where you have a contact

- ✓ Have a conversation with that potential partner about the possibility of joining forces to improve the revenue of both companies by expanding the offerings.
- ✓ Determine the need for a contract.
- ✓ Utilize partnership-termination points in your agreement, and identify the time for referrals, commissions, and payments.
- ✓ Clearly state which partner owns the client database, contact records or any other pertinent information and whether this is shared.
- ✓ In cases of guarantees or warranties provided to the client, identify the responsible party under various circumstances applicable to the partnership.
- ✓ Communicate to the client(s) who will be managing the product/service so the reputation of both firms is intact.

Working with other organizations to build and sustain your client list is a tremendous step forward. Not only do partners assist in growing your business, but they protect against economic fluctuations and can even provide ideas for new products or services.

A good approach to adopt is to view every person you meet in your community—from the grocery store to the repair shop and in between—as either a potential client or a potential partner. The effect of this perspective will be immediate. You may find yourself greeting others with a smile, being a little more patient while in the waiting line, or giving unsolicited offers of help those around you.

Call it good karma, good business or being a good person, it's going to come around to you when you need it most.

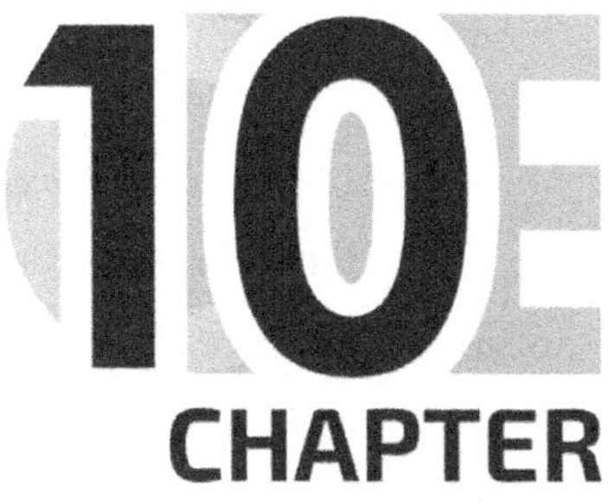

Even when I became editor of Vogue-America, I kept moonlighting at a garment store.

Mary McFadden

Chapter Ten: Moonlighting Your Way to Success

Madonna famously said that even when she had sixty million in the bank, she was always afraid the money was going to go away, and that she wouldn't be able to earn it again. That attitude drove her to work herself harder (and those around her just as hard) well after it was necessary. The memory of sleeping on the floor and taking handouts from others was always in the back of her mind.

To a lesser degree, the back-of-the-mind fear for many consultants is that the projects will dry up and then they will need to go back to work. It's why you may keep your day job for a period of time, or forever, but continue to moonlight after their day job is over.

"I was waiting for the fear to subside," is what my friend in the outsourced sales business confided. **But what she, and so many other**

consultants, discovered is that the fear doesn't really leave. It's replaced by confidence in client demand, the growing bank account and "the ability to sleep at night," according to Bryan Kelley.

Consulting is not mutually exclusive to working at Starbucks or Sony or Wal-Mart, or being a stay-at-home mom. Consulting is defined by leveraging your skill set and knowledge in a capacity that works for *you.* And if that means your time allocation for the consulting job is Tuesday and Thursday evenings, you communicate that availability to prospective clients. **If your prospective clients really value the service you provide, they will adjust their schedules to accommodate yours**.

The best of both worlds

Think about it. We adjust our schedules for the UPS deliveryman, the carpet cleaner, and the ever-present cable installer, and yet, *we are paying them*! The consulting business is no different, other than it's your service that's being provided.

Take Erika Spry, who was approached by one of her clients, a large, medical services company with multiple locations, to become the general manager. **She was interested, but unwilling to drop a few of her long-time, core clients in the restaurant industry**. Beyond the income and safety net it provided, she genuinely loves the food and beverage industry. At the same time, the new opportunity was an exciting challenge she didn't want to pass up.

"I spoke frankly with the owners [of the medical services company] and we came to a very easy agreement," she explained. She would transition to full-time employment after a period of months, giving her time to complete the majority of her projects, but she wasn't required to give up her selected clients, nor shut the doors of her well respected small business.

"I have the best of both worlds," said Erika. **"I keep my foot in the door with several key clients but have the ability to pursue a new job which holds a lot of exciting possibilities."**

In a time of uncertainty, with the prospect of another recession, Erika wants to keep her options open.

So, does Dr. Satava, who juggles one of the more complex schedules I've seen. He keeps his clients happy, avoids conflicts of interest and manages his routine by following a few guidelines.

"First, I check my conflicts with my primary employer, then go down the list," he explained. Second, "I consult on university time, not on government time." This is because the government is buying a percentage of his time from the university, paying the university directly.

The university contract permits the university to recoup his salary and benefits proportional to the time he works with the government.

"There are many consultants who can leave government, set up their own company, and then consult for a fee just as I do, but without the conflict-of-interest problems." But because Dr. Satava continues to perform surgeries and other duties pertaining to his medical profession, and he has no desire to leave this work, he is a special case.

When it comes to private clients, Dr. Satava may accept money for travel and expenses, but he isn't allowed to accept fees. This is done to avoid the conflict-of-interest issues. It also relieves him of concern over his clients' time-to-market goals.

"I'm presently consulting with an established, traditional medical instrument company," he continued. "With the rapid discovery of new technologies, they are concerned about obsolescence." Since they are very successful and have been able to be early adopters of new technology and able to quickly commercialize new technologies, Satava's consulting brings technology advancements to his clients earlier in their product development lifecycle, and gives them the confidence to develop a technology sooner than they would otherwise.

"Also, I tell them of the competing technologies that may make their product irrelevant (usually from a different field)." This gives his client a tremendous head start on the competition."

Mike Konesky whole-heartedly agrees with consulting on the side while having a full-time job.

"Obviously, if you don't have any conflict-of-interest issues," he says, "and ensure that there would be no negative impact such as expected delivery, results, hours billed and the like on the primary job, it's fine."

The best part of this hybrid combination is that it applies to so many vocations. In fact, Mike has seen "employers respond especially favorably if it enhances the overall skills of an employee." So, if the primary job is not affected adversely, why not?! Have fun, and generate more income.

Natural Job Extension

Not surprisingly, employees are reluctant to approach their existing employer about working on the side. The situation may depend on your existing role within the company, the time and mental energy that you might devote to a consulting project (and conversely, away from thinking about your main job), and the industry norms. It's standard for doctors to have consulting projects on the side, even if the doctor is in private practice, and particularly when working for a teaching institution. It's also the norm for part-time workers to have second or even third jobs. The difference between the two is low-skilled jobs versus high-skilled jobs.

Take the case of Janel Ecker, founder and CEO of landscape consulting firm Terra Firma Landscape Design in Maple Valley, Washington. She graduated from design school and was hired by a local boutique nursery serving mixed residential neighborhoods with both rural land properties and custom designed homes.

After a few years of working at the nursery, she noticed some regular nursery clients couldn't have their landscaping needs met during the spring season.

"In Seattle, the planting season can be very short, so the rush to get a design and planting is crazy," she told me. Janel saw an opportunity and took it.

"I approached the manager of the nursery and offered to take the extra customers off her hands," she began, reasoning to her boss that "we'd rather have happy customers that are satisfied than have them leave us and search for landscape design at another nursery." The logic held, since the consultant often recommends where to purchase plants, in addition to what type. Some clients have the landscape designers make purchases on behalf of themselves, and that's money that's walking out the door to a nursery where the consultant already has an established relationship.

Janel's personalized service was so successful she had a full client list of her own within several months. Her business has continued to increase three-fold for two years running, giving her enough revenue to complete an addition on her home and a full remodel on the original portion. During the fourth year, Janel left the nursery to concentrate on her business full-time but still receives referrals from the staff as well as other clients. As a consultant (and not nursery owner) she always refers and sources plants from her original employer. They have both benefited from this relationship, revenue and profits increasing over the years. Furthermore, it didn't require paperwork to get started.

Approaching Your Boss

You're not the first person to suggest cutting down on lost client services or hedging against downtime during the slow months of the year. Why not craft the business case for one consulting niche as you maintain your primary job? You might be surprised and find that your boss wants you to consult full-time— for him or her. Here are a few of the things that you should do before approaching your boss:

- **Consider the Demand and Trends**

Some consulting services are built around weather (think travel) and in demographic areas (think Vermont and fall weddings, or summer and tropical weddings). This might open the door to working with your boss around seasonal slowdowns or rush periods, where you can assist in the busy times, such as Janel aiding her nursery. Alternatively, you could take more time off during a slow period to build up your own business.

- **Provide the Business Case Justification**

If you can answer yes to the following questions, you are prepared to have a conversation with your boss:

- ✓ Does the business case make sense for the employer?
- ✓ Does it take away current business from the employer?
- ✓ Does conflict of interest exist?
- ✓ Does it hurt the reputation of the employer in any way?
- ✓ Are you using the employer's intellectual property and/or process in your work?
- ✓ If so, do you need to reimburse the employer for usage, or find a way to avoid using employer information?
- ✓ What guarantee does the employer have that you won't bad-mouth the employer's own services?

- **Cement Your Case with Time Commitment**

Assist your business case by providing a time commitment for continued service to your employer, on either a weekly or monthly basis. This shows a willingness to continue to be a part of team in situations when a transition is required. Even if your services aren't required, you've ended on a positive note by leaving the door open for additional work —just in case‖ your employer needs your skills in the future.

Ten Consulting Vocations

You might have lived overseas, worked in a printing plant, or been a part of a youth organization that provided new housing to underprivileged families. Whether your passions lie with animals, social causes or travel and leisure, a consulting vocation almost surely exists. And if it doesn't, now is your time to create a niche.

1. **Cultural Consultant**: consult to clients looking to do business in a new part of the world.
2. **Editorial Consultant**: consult to an authors or movie studios about a piece of fiction or nonfiction that requires a unique perspective.
3. **Foreign Aid Worker Consultant**: consult with dentists, doctors and other service providers to gain funding and provide service in a foreign country.
4. **Social Cause Consultant**: consult to companies looking to make a difference for a social cause.
5. **Franchise Consulting**: consult to individuals or organizations that would like to sell to, or work with, franchises and don't know who to get started.
6. **Medical Resource Consultant**: consult to medical teaching institutions that are always needing to find new sources of education, influence, and fundraising.

7. **Regulatory Affairs Consultant**: consult to clients seeking to accelerate efforts within a highly regulated industry.
8. **Health Management Consultant**: consult to a large corporation about physical fitness goals by planning, implementing, and managing programs.
9. **Disabilities Programs Consultant**: consult with agencies and private organizations to assess and improve disabilities programs, from hiring to job descriptions and environment.
10. **Green Consultant**: consult on a single aspect of being environmentally green based on your own skill set and background.

Chapter 10 Summary

- ✓ Consider staying at your existing job and starting your consulting business with the full knowledge of your employer.
- ✓ Identify the seasonal or industry up and down times.
- ✓ Create a business case for a consulting job outside your employer, either as an individual consultant *back* to the employer, or assisting the employer with extra projects.
- ✓ Establish the ground rules for working alongside your primary employer.

This last option of working outside the confines of your day job with the full-knowledge and perhaps even support of your employer may open another door to your career that was previously closed. Mike

Konesky related that one of the biggest career breaks occurred when he voiced to his boss he had ideas that could and should be used, and if the employer wasn't interested in doing so, then it was an opportunity he might need to pursue—on his own. His boss was so impressed with Mike's ability to spot an opportunity that he was given more responsibility, an increase in pay and the full ability to follow-through on his ideas.

You are ready to make a change in your life, to take that first step towards earning additional income, and to prepare yourself and your family members or the ups and downs of the economy. If you haven't already begun the process, do so now. Use the talents and knowledge you have earned to create the life you have dreamed about. And when you do, tell me about it. I'd love to feature you in my next article, blog or book.

Appendix: Additional Resources

- Consulting-only networking forums open to all include the International Consultant Networking Association (www.icna-net.org).
- **Networking forums**: look for networking forums designed around your demographic. If you are a female consultant in the Washington, DC area, you might try www.consultingwomen.com.
- **Independent Human Resources** Consultants Association (www.ihrca.com).
- **Advertising consulting** networking includes the UConsultUs, (www.uconsultus.com), an advertising resource for independent consultants seeking international clients.
- **American Consultants League** (www.grasmick.com/acl.htm) is a network of consultants in a variety of disciplines that provides resource materials.
- **Society of Professional Consultants** (SPC), (www.spconsultants.org). The non-profit holds monthly meetings for consultants and provides referral services to the public.

ACKNOWLEDGEMENTS

The pearls of wisdom I've held on to, remembered, and shared in this book have come from a great many sources.

First, my father, who started schooling me in the art of business. Kermit Yensen, the first VP of marketing who saved me the time and money of attending Harvard as he provided me with many marketing models, theories, and product-launch strategies he learned during his time at the school. Melody Haller, a guru of public relations in San Francisco, and taught me the majority of what I know about working with the media. Tim Bajarin for giving me sage advice. Tim Krause, who took a chance on a young, unknown, unproven but passionate consultant. Finally, my thanks and gratitude goes out to David Johnstone, an attorney by day and a consulting editor by night. This book is much improved by his red pen, suggestions and support. Thank you all.

ABOUT THE AUTHOR

Sarah Gerdes founded BMG, a partner development consultancy, and is credited with establishing the niche of outsourced partner development as a recognized field. She sold her first client to Microsoft at 27, one year after founding her consultancy. Her clients have included Fortune 500 companies, governments, and private companies alike. Her successes have been featured in *Fortune* Magazine, *Inc., Entrepreneur*, and the *Economist*, and she was the first partner consultant asked to speak at Harvard, MIT, Stanford and other prestigious institutions. Her thirteen books have been published in three languages and sixteen countries, and she now serves as a board member to private and non-profit entities.

BOOKS IN PRINT BY SARAH GERDES

Non-Fiction

Sue Kim: The Authorized Biography

Author Straight Talk: the possibilities, pitfalls, how-to's and tribal knowledge from someone who knows

Navigating the Partnership Maze: Creating Alliances that Work (McGraw-Hill) (English and Chinese)

Fiction:

Global Deadline
In a Moment
Danielle Grant Series
- Made for Me (Book 1)
- Destined for You (Book 2)
- Meant to Be (Book 3)

A Convenient Date
Chambers Series
- Chambers (book 1)
- Chambers: *The Spirit Warrior* (book 2)

Incarnation Series
- Incarnation
- Incarnation: *The Cube Master* (book 2)

AUTHOR RESOURCES

Instagram: sarahgerdes_author
Facebook: sarah gerdes author
Web site: www.sarahgerdes.com
YouTube: Sarah Gerdes Author
01142018

Index

Made in the USA
Columbia, SC
07 February 2021